A Selection From The Lyrical Poems Of Robert Herrick

Robert Herrick

Edited by Francis Turner Palgrave

A SELECTION FROM THE LYRICAL POEMS OF ROBERT HERRICK

BY
Robert Herrick
Edited by Francis Turner Palgrave

A SelectionFrom The Lyrical Poems Of Robert Herrick
Arranged with introduction by Francis Turner Palgrave

PREFACE

ROBERT HERRICK - Born 1591 : Died 1674

Those who most admire the Poet from whose many pieces a selection only is here offered, will, it is probable, feel most strongly (with the Editor) that excuse is needed for an attempt of an obviously presumptuous nature. The choice made by any selector invites challenge: the admission, perhaps, of some poems, the absence of more, will be censured:--Whilst others may wholly condemn the process, in virtue of an argument not unfrequently advanced of late, that a writer's judgment on his own work is to be considered final. And his book to be taken as he left it, or left altogether; a literal reproduction of the original text being occasionally included in this requirement.

If poetry were composed solely for her faithful band of true lovers and true students, such a facsimile as that last indicated would have claims irresistible; but if the first and last object of this, as of the other Fine Arts, may be defined in language borrowed from a different range of thought, as 'the greatest pleasure of the greatest number,' it is certain that less stringent forms of reproduction are required and justified. The great majority of readers cannot bring either leisure or taste, or information sufficient to take them through a large mass (at any rate) of ancient verse, not even if it be Spenser's or Milton's. Manners and modes of speech, again, have changed; and much that was admissible centuries since, or at least sought admission, has now, by a law against which protest is idle, lapsed into the indecorous. Even unaccustomed forms of spelling are an effort to the eye;--a kind of friction, which diminishes the ease and enjoyment of the reader.

These hindrances and clogs, of very diverse nature, cannot be disregarded by Poetry. In common with everything which aims at human benefit, she must work not only for the 'faithful': she has also the duty of 'conversion.' Like a messenger from heaven, it is hers to inspire, to console, to elevate: to convert the world, in a word, to herself. Every rough place that slackens her footsteps must be made smooth; nor, in this Art, need there be fear that the way will ever be vulgarized by too much ease, nor that she will be loved less by the elect, for being loved more widely.

Passing from these general considerations, it is true that a selection framed in conformity with them, especially if one of our older poets be concerned, parts with a certain portion of the pleasure which poetry may confer. A writer is most thoroughly to be judged by the whole of what he printed. A selector inevitably holds too despotic a position over his author. The frankness of speech which we have abandoned is an interesting evidence how the tone of manners changes. The poet's own spelling and punctuation bear, or may bear, a gleam of his personality. But such last drops of pleasure are the reward of fully-formed taste; and fully-formed taste cannot be reached without full knowledge. This, we have noticed, most readers cannot bring. Hence, despite all drawbacks, an anthology may have its place. A book which tempts many to read a little, will guide some to that more profound and loving study of which the result is, the full accomplishment of the poet's mission.

We have, probably, no poet to whom the reasons here advanced to justify the invidious task of selection apply more fully and forcibly than to Herrick. Highly as he is to be rated among our lyrists, no one who reads through his fourteen hundred pieces can reasonably doubt that whatever may have been the influences, --wholly unknown to us,--which determined the contents of his volume, severe taste was not one of them. PECAT FORTITER:--his exquisite directness and simplicity of speech repeatedly take such form that the book cannot be offered to a very large number of those readers who would most enjoy it. The spelling is at once arbitrary and obsolete. Lastly, the complete reproduction of the original text, with explanatory notes, edited by Mr Grosart, supplies materials equally full and interesting for those who may, haply, be allured by this little book to master one of our most attractive poets in his integrity.

A Selection From The Lyrical Poems Of Robert Herrick

In Herrick's single own edition of HESPERIDES and NOBLE NUMBERS, but little arrangement is traceable: nor have we more than a few internal signs of date in composition. It would hence be unwise to attempt grouping the poems on a strict plan: and the divisions under which they are here ranged must be regarded rather as progressive aspects of a landscape than as territorial demarcations. Pieces bearing on the poet as such are placed first; then, those vaguely definable as of idyllic character, 'his girls,' epigrams, poems on natural objects, on character and life; lastly, a few in his religious vein. For the text, although reference has been made to the original of 1647-8, Mr Grosart's excellent reprint has been mainly followed. And to that edition this book is indebted for many valuable exegetical notes, kindly placed at the Editor's disposal. But for much fuller elucidation both of words and allusions, and of the persons mentioned, readers are referred to Mr Grosart's volumes, which (like the same scholar's 'Sidney' and 'Donne'), for the first time give Herrick a place among books not printed only, but edited.

Robert Herrick's personal fate is in one point like Shakespeare's. We know or seem to know them both, through their works, with singular intimacy. But with this our knowledge substantially ends. No private letter of Shakespeare, no record of his conversation, no account of the circumstances in which his writings were published, remains: hardly any statement how his greatest contemporaries ranked him. A group of Herrick's youthful letters on business has, indeed, been preserved; of his life and studies, of his reputation during his own time, almost nothing. For whatever facts affectionate diligence could now gather. Readers are referred to Mr Grosart's 'Introduction.' But if, to supplement the picture, inevitably imperfect, which this gives, we turn to Herrick's own book, we learn little, biographically, except the names of a few friends,--that his general sympathies were with the Royal cause,--and that he wearied in Devonshire for London. So far as is known, he published but this one volume, and that, when not far from his sixtieth year. Some pieces may be traced in earlier collections; some few carry ascertainable dates; the rest lie over a period of near forty years, during a great portion of which we have no distinct account where Herrick lived, or what were his employments. We know that he shone with Ben Jonson and the wits at the nights and suppers of those gods of our glorious early literature: we may fancy him at Beaumanor, or Houghton, with his uncle and cousins, keeping a Leicestershire Christmas in the Manor-house: or, again, in some sweet southern county with Julia and Anthea, Corinna and Dianeme by his side (familiar then by other names now never to be remembered), sitting merry, but with just the sadness of one who hears sweet music, in some meadow among his favourite flowers of spring-time;--there, or 'where the rose lingers latest.' .... But 'the dream, the fancy,' is all that Time has spared us. And if it be curious that his contemporaries should have left so little record of this delightful poet and (as we should infer from the book) genial- hearted man, it is not less so that the single first edition should have satisfied the seventeenth century, and that, before the present, notices of Herrick should be of the rarest occurrence.

The artist's 'claim to exist' is, however, always far less to be looked for in his life, than in his art, upon the secret of which the fullest biography can tell us little--as little, perhaps, as criticism can analyse its charm. But there are few of our poets who stand less in need than Herrick of commentaries of this description,--in which too often we find little more than a dull or florid prose version of what the author has given us admirably in verse. Apart from obsolete words or allusions, Herrick is the best commentator upon Herrick. A few lines only need therefore here be added, aiming rather to set forth his place in the sequence of English poets, and especially in regard to those near his own time, than to point out in detail beauties which he unveils in his own way, and so most durably and delightfully.

When our Muses, silent or sick for a century and more after Chaucer's death, during the years of war and revolution, reappeared, they brought with them foreign modes of art, ancient and contemporary, in the forms of which they began to set to music the new material which the age supplied. At the very outset, indeed, the moralizing philosophy which has characterized the English from the beginning of our national history, appears in the writers of the troubled times lying between the last regnal years of Henry VIII and the first of his great daughter. But with the happier hopes of Elizabeth's accession, poetry was once more distinctly followed, not only as a means of conveying thought, but as a Fine Art. And hence something constrained and artificial blends with the freshness of the Elizabethan literature. For its great underlying elements it necessarily reverts to those embodied in our own earlier poets, Chaucer above all, to whom, after barely one hundred and fifty years, men looked up as a father of song: but in points of style and treatment, the poets of the sixteenth century lie under a double external influence--that of the poets of Greece and Rome (known either in their own tongues or by translation), and that of the modern literatures which had themselves undergone the same classical impulse. Italy was the source most regarded during the more strictly Elizabethan period; whence its lyrical poetry and the dramatic in a less degree, are coloured much less by pure and severe classicalism with its closeness to reality, than by the allegorical and elaborate style, fancy and fact curiously blended, which had been generated in Italy under the peculiar and local circumstances of her pilgrimage in literature and art from the age of Dante onwards. Whilst that influence lasted, such brilliant pictures of actual life, such directness, movement, and simplicity in style, as Chaucer often shows, were not yet again attainable: and although satire, narrative, the poetry of reflection, were meanwhile not wholly unknown, yet they only appear in force at the close of this period. And then also the pressure of political and religious strife, veiled in poetry during the greater part of Elizabeth's actual reign under the forms of pastoral and allegory, again imperiously breaks in upon the gracious but somewhat slender and artificial fashions of England's Helicon: the DIVOM NUMEN, SEDESQUE QUIETAE which, in some degree the Elizabethan poets offer, disappear; until filling the central years of the seventeenth century we reach an age as barren for inspiration of new song as the Wars of the Roses; although the great survivors from earlier years mask this sterility;--masking also the revolution in poetical manner and matter which we can see secretly preparing in the later 'Cavalier' poets, but which was not clearly recognised before the time of Dryden's culmination.

In the period here briefly sketched, what is Herrick's portion? His verse is eminent for sweet and gracious fluency; this is a real note of the 'Elizabethan' poets. His subjects are frequently pastoral, with a classical tinge, more or less slight, infused; his language, though not free from exaggeration, is generally free from intellectual conceits and distortion, and is eminent throughout for a youthful NAIVETE. Such, also, are qualities of the latter sixteenth century literature. But if these characteristics might lead us to call Herrick 'the last of the Elizabethans,' born out of due time, the differences between him and them are not less marked. Herrick's directness of speech is accompanied by an equally clear and simple presentment of his thought;

we have, perhaps, no poet who writes more consistently and earnestly with his eye upon his subject. An allegorical or mystical treatment is alien from him: he handles awkwardly the few traditional fables which he introduces. He is also wholly free from Italianizing tendencies: his classicalism even is that of an English student,--of a schoolboy, indeed, if he be compared with a Jonson or a Milton. Herrick's personal eulogies on his friends and others, further, witness to the extension of the field of poetry after Elizabeth's age;--in which his enthusiastic geniality, his quick and easy transitions of subject, have also little precedent.

If, again, we compare Herrick's book with those of his fellow-poets for a hundred years before, very few are the traces which he gives of imitation, or even of study. During the long interval between Herrick's entrance on his Cambridge and his clerical careers (an interval all but wholly obscure to us), it is natural to suppose that he read, at any rate, his Elizabethan predecessors: yet (beyond those general similarities already noticed) the Editor can find no positive proof of familiarity. Compare Herrick with Marlowe, Greene, Breton, Drayton, or other pretty pastoralists of the HELICON--his general and radical unlikeness is what strikes us; whilst he is even more remote from the passionate intensity of Sidney and Shakespeare, the Italian graces of Spenser, the pensive beauty of PARTHENOPHIL, of DIELLA, of FIDESSA, of the HECATOMPATHIA and the TEARS OF FANCY.

Nor is Herrick's resemblance nearer to many of the contemporaries who have been often grouped with him. He has little in common with the courtly elegance, the learned polish, which too rarely redeem commonplace and conceits in Carew, Habington, Lovelace, Cowley, or Waller. Herrick has his CONCETTI also: but they are in him generally true plays of fancy; he writes throughout far more naturally than these lyrics, who, on the other hand, in their unfrequent successes reach a more complete and classical form of expression. Thus, when Carew speaks of an aged fair one

> When beauty, youth, and all sweets leave her,
> Love may return, but lovers never!

Cowley, of his mistress--

Love in her sunny eyes does basking play,
Love walks the pleasant mazes of her hair:

or take Lovelace, 'To Lucasta,' Waller, in his 'Go, lovely rose,'--we have a finish and condensation which Herrick hardly attains; a literary quality alien from his 'woodnotes wild,' which may help us to understand the very small appreciation he met from his age. He had 'a pretty pastoral gale of fancy,' said Phillips, cursorily dismissing Herrick in his THEATRUM: not suspecting how inevitably artifice and mannerism, if fashionable for awhile, pass into forgetfulness, whilst the simple cry of Nature partake in her permanence.

Donne and Marvell, stronger men, leave also no mark on our poet. The elaborate thought, the metrical harshness of the first, could find no counterpart in Herrick; whilst Marvell, beyond him in imaginative power, though twisting it too often into contortion and excess, appears to have been little known as a lyrist then:-- as, indeed, his great merits have never reached anything like due popular recognition. Yet Marvell's natural description is nearer Herrick's in felicity and insight than any of the poets named above. Nor, again, do we trace anything of Herbert or Vaughan in Herrick's NOBLE NUMBERS, which, though unfairly judged if held insincere, are obviously far distant from the intense conviction, the depth and inner fervour of his high-toned contemporaries.

It is among the great dramatists of this age that we find the only English influences palpably operative on this singularly original writer. The greatest, in truth, is wholly absent: and it is remarkable that although Herrick may have joined in the wit-contests and genialities of the literary clubs in London soon after Shakespeare's death, and certainly lived in friendship with some who had known him, yet his name is never mentioned in the poetical commemorations of the HESPERIDES. In Herrick, echoes from Fletcher's idyllic pieces in the FAITHFUL SHEPHERDESS are faintly traceable; from his songs, 'Hear what Love can do,' and 'The lusty Spring,' more distinctly. But to Ben Jonson, whom Herrick addresses as his patron saint in song, and ranks on the highest list of his friends, his obligations are much more perceptible. In fact, Jonson's non-dramatic poetry,--the EPIGRAMS and FOREST of 1616, the UNDERWOODS of 1641, (he died in 1637),-- supply models, generally admirable in point of art, though of very unequal merit in their execution and contents, of the principal forms under which we may range Herrick's HESPERIDES. The graceful love-song, the celebration of feasts and wit, the encomia of friends, the epigram as then understood, are all here represented: even Herrick's vein in natural description is prefigured in the odes to Penshurst and Sir Robert Wroth, of 1616. And it is in the religious pieces of the NOBLE NUMBERS, for which Jonson afforded the least copious precedents, that, as a rule, Herrick is least successful.

Even if we had not the verses on his own book, (the most noteworthy of which are here printed as PREFATORY,) in proof that Herrick was no careless singer, but a true artist, working with conscious knowledge of his art, we might have inferred the fact from the choice of Jonson as his model. That great poet, as Clarendon justly remarked, had 'judgment to order and govern fancy, rather than excess of fancy: his productions being slow and upon deliberation.' No writer could be better fitted for the guidance of one so fancy-free as Herrick; to whom the curb, in the old phrase, was more needful than the spur, and whose invention, more fertile and varied than Jonson's, was ready at once to fill up the moulds of form provided. He does this with a lively facility, contrasting much with the evidence of labour in his master's work. Slowness and deliberation are the last qualities suggested by Herrick. Yet it may be doubted whether the volatile ease, the effortless grace, the wild bird-like fluency with which he

> Scatters his loose notes in the waste of air

are not, in truth, the results of exquisite art working in co- operation with the gifts of nature. The various readings which our few remaining manuscripts or printed versions have supplied to Mr Grosart's 'Introduction,' attest the minute and curious care with which Herrick polished and strengthened his own work: his airy facility, his seemingly spontaneous melodies, as with Shelley--his counterpart in pure lyrical art within this century --were earned by conscious labour; perfect freedom was begotten of perfect art;--nor, indeed, have excellence and permanence any other parent.

With the error that regards Herrick as a careless singer is closely twined that which ranks him in the school of that master of elegant pettiness who has usurped and abused the name Anacreon; as a mere light-hearted writer of pastorals, a gay and frivolous Renaissance amourist. He has indeed those elements: but with them is joined the seriousness of an age which knew that the light mask of classicalism and bucolic allegory could be worn only as an ornament, and that life held much deeper and further- reaching issues than were visible to the narrow horizons within which Horace or Martial circumscribed the range of their art. Between the most intensely poetical, and so, greatest, among the French poets of this century, and Herrick, are many points of likeness. He too, with Alfred de Musset, might have said

>   Quoi que nous puissions faire,
>   Je souffre; il est trop tard; le monde s'est fait vieux.
>   Une immense esperance a traverse la terre;
>   Malgre nous vers le ciel il faut lever les yeux.

Indeed, Herrick's deepest debt to ancient literature lies not in the models which he directly imitated, nor in the Anacreontic tone which with singular felicity he has often taken. These are common to many writers with him:--nor will he who cannot learn more from the great ancient world ever rank among poets of high order, or enter the innermost sanctuary of art. But, the power to describe men and things as the poet sees them with simple sincerity, insight, and grace: to paint scenes and imaginations as perfect organic wholes;--carrying with it the gift to clothe each picture, as if by unerring instinct, in fit metrical form, giving to each its own music; beginning without affectation, and rounding off without effort;-- the power, in a word, to leave simplicity, sanity, and beauty as the last impressions lingering on our minds, these gifts are at once the true bequest of classicalism, and the reason why (until modern effort equals them) the study of that Hellenic and Latin poetry in which these gifts are eminent above all other literatures yet created, must be essential. And it is success in precisely these excellences which is here claimed for Herrick. He is classical in the great and eternal sense of the phrase: and much more so, probably, than he was himself aware of. No poet in fact is so far from dwelling in a past or foreign world: it is the England, if not of 1648, at least of his youth, in which he lives and moves and loves: his Bucolics show no trace of Sicily: his Anthea and Julia wear no 'buckles of the purest gold,' nor have anything about them foreign to Middlesex or Devon. Herrick's imagination has no far horizons: like Burns and Crabbe fifty years since, or Barnes (that exquisite and neglected pastoralist of fair Dorset, perfect within his narrower range as Herrick) to-day, it is his own native land only which he sees and paints: even the fairy world in which, at whatever inevitable interval, he is second to Shakespeare, is pure English; or rather, his elves live in an elfin county of their own, and are all but severed from humanity. Within that greater circle of Shakespeare, where Oberon and Ariel and their fellows move, aiding or injuring mankind, and reflecting human life in a kind of unconscious parody, Herrick cannot walk: and it may have been due to his good sense and true feeling for art, that here, where resemblance might have seemed probable, he borrows nothing from MIDSUMMER NIGHT'S DREAM or TEMPEST. if we are moved by the wider range of Byron's or Shelley's sympathies, there is a charm, also, in this sweet insularity of Herrick; a narrowness perhaps, yet carrying with it a healthful reality absent from the vapid and artificial 'cosmopolitanism' that did such wrong on Goethe's genius. If he has not the exotic blooms and strange odours which poets who derive from literature show in their conservatories, Herrick has the fresh breeze and thyme-bed fragrance of open moorland, the grace and greenery of English meadows: with Homer and Dante, he too shares the strength and inspiration which come from touch of a man's native soil.

What has been here sketched is not planned so much as a criticism in form on Herrick's poetry as an attempt to seize his relations to his predecessors and contemporaries. If we now tentatively inquire what place may be assigned to him in our literature at large, Herrick has no single lyric to show equal, in pomp of music, brilliancy of diction, or elevation of sentiment to some which Spenser before, Milton in his own time, Dryden and Gray, Wordsworth and Shelley, since have given us. Nor has he, as already noticed, the peculiar finish and reserve (if the phrase may be allowed) traceable, though rarely, in Ben Jonson and others of the seventeenth century. He does not want passion; yet his passion wants concentration: it is too ready, also, to dwell on externals: imagination with him generally appears clothed in forms of fancy. Among his contemporaries, take Crashaw's 'Wishes': Sir J. Beaumont's elegy on his child Gervase: take Bishop King's 'Surrender':

> My once-dear Love!--hapless, that I no more
> Must call thee so. . . . The rich affection's store
> That fed our hopes, lies now exhaust and spent,

Like sums of treasure unto bankrupts lent:--
We that did nothing study but the way
To love each other, with which thoughts the day
Rose with delight to us, and with them set,
Must learn the hateful art, how to forget!
--Fold back our arms, take home our fruitless loves,
That must new fortunes try, like turtle doves
Dislodged from their haunts. We must in tears
Unwind a love knit up in many years.
In this one kiss I here surrender thee
Back to thyself: so thou again art free:-

take eight lines by some old unknown Northern singer:

When I think on the happy days
   I spent wi' you, my dearie,
And now what lands between us lie,
   How can I be but eerie!

How slow ye move, ye heavy hours,
   As ye were wae and weary!
It was na sae ye glinted by
   When I was wi' my dearie:--

   --O! there is an intensity here, a note of passion beyond the deepest of Herrick's. This tone (whether from temperament or circumstance or scheme of art), is wanting to the HESPERIDES and NOBLE NUMBERS: nor does Herrick's lyre, sweet and varied as it is, own that purple chord, that more inwoven harmony, possessed by poets of greater depth and splendour,--by Shakespeare and Milton often, by Spenser more rarely. But if we put aside these 'greater gods' of song, with Sidney,--in the Editor's judgment Herrick's mastery (to use a brief expression), both over Nature and over Art, clearly assigns to him the first place as lyrical poet, in the strict and pure sense of the phrase, among all who flourished during the interval between Henry V and a hundred years since. Single pieces of equal, a few of higher, quality, we have, indeed, meanwhile received, not only from the master-singers who did not confine themselves to the Lyric, but from many poets--some the unknown contributors to our early anthologies, then Jonson, Marvell, Waller, Collins, and others, with whom we reach the beginning of the wider sweep which lyrical poetry has since taken. Yet, looking at the whole work, not at the selected jewels, of this great and noble multitude, Herrick, as lyrical poet strictly, offers us by far the most homogeneous, attractive, and varied treasury. No one else among lyrists within the period defined, has such unfailing freshness: so much variety within the sphere prescribed to himself: such closeness to nature, whether in description or in feeling: such easy fitness in language: melody so unforced and delightful. His dull pages are much less frequent: he has more lines, in his own phrase, 'born of the royal blood': the

> Inflata rore non Achaico verba

are rarer with him: although superficially mannered, nature is so much nearer to him, that far fewer of his pieces have lost vitality and interest through adherence to forms of feeling or fashions of thought now obsolete. A Roman contemporary is described by the younger Pliny in words very appropriate to Herrick: who, in fact, if Greek in respect of his method and style, in the contents of his poetry displays the 'frankness of nature and vivid sense of life' which criticism assigns as marks of the great Roman poets. FACIT VERSUS, QUALES CATULLUS AUT CALVUS. QUANTUM ILLIS LEPORIS, DULCEDINIS, AMARITUDINIS AMORIS! INSERIT SANE, SED DATA OPERA, MOLLIBUS LENIBUSQUE DURIUSCULOS QUOSDAM; ET HOC, QUASI CATULLUS AUT CALVUS. Many pieces have been, here refused admittance, whether from coarseness of phrase or inferior value: yet these are rarely defective in the lyrical art, which, throughout the writer's work, is so simple and easy as almost to escape notice through its very excellence. In one word, Herrick, in a rare and special sense, is unique.

To these qualities we may, perhaps, ascribe the singular neglect which, so far as we may infer, he met with in his own age, and certainly in the century following. For the men of the Restoration period he was too natural, too purely poetical: he had not the learned polish, the political allusion, the tone of the city, the didactic turn, which were then and onwards demanded from poetry. In the next age, no tradition consecrated his name; whilst writers of a hundred years before were then too remote for familiarity, and not remote enough for reverence. Moving on to our own time, when some justice has at length been conceded to him, Herrick has to meet the great rivalry of the poets who, from Burns and Cowper to Tennyson, have widened and deepened the lyrical sphere, making it at once on the one hand more intensely personal, on the other, more free and picturesque in the range of problems dealt with: whilst at the same time new and richer lyrical forms, harmonies more intricate and seven-fold, have been created by them, as in Hellas during her golden age of song, to embody ideas and emotions unknown or unexpressed under Tudors and Stuarts. To this latter superiority Herrick would, doubtless, have bowed, as he bowed before Ben Jonson's genius. 'Rural ditties,' and 'oaten flute' cannot bear the competition of the full modern orchestra. Yet this author need not fear! That exquisite: and lofty pleasure which it is the first and the last aim of all true art to give, must, by its own nature, be lasting also. As the eyesight fluctuates, and gives the advantage to different colours in turn, so to the varying moods of the mind the same beauty does not always seem equally beautiful. Thus from the 'purple light' of our later poetry there are hours in which we may look to the daffodil and rose-tints of Herrick's old Arcadia, for refreshment and delight. And the pleasure which he gives is as eminently wholesome as pleasurable. Like the holy river of Virgil, to the souls who drink of him, Herrick offers 'securos latices.' He is conspicuously free from many of the maladies incident to his art. Here is no overstrain, no spasmodic cry, so wire-drawn analysis or sensational rhetoric, no music without sense, no mere second-hand literary inspiration, no mannered archaism:--above all, no sickly sweetness, no subtle, unhealthy affectation. Throughout his work, whether when it is strong, or in the less worthy portions, sanity, sincerity, simplicity, lucidity, are everywhere the characteristics of Herrick: in these, not in his pretty Pagan masquerade, he shows the note,--the only genuine note,--of Hellenic descent. Hence, through whatever changes and fashions poetry may pass, her true lovers he is likely to 'please now, and please for long.' His verse, in the words of a poet greater than himself, is of that quality which 'adds sunlight to daylight'; which is able to 'make the happy happier.' He will, it may be hoped, carry to the many Englands across the seas, east and west, pictures of English life exquisite in truth and grace:--to the more fortunate inhabitants (as they must perforce hold themselves!) of the old country, her image, as she was two centuries since, will live in the 'golden apples' of the West, offered to us by this sweet singer of Devonshire. We have greater poets, not a few; none more faithful to nature as he saw her, none more perfect in his art;--none, more companionable:--

    F. T. P. Dec. 1876

CHRYSOMELA

A SELECTION FROM THE LYRICAL POEMS OF ROBERT HERRICK

** PREFATORY **

1

THE ARGUMENT OF HIS BOOK

I sing of brooks, of blossoms, birds, and bowers,
Of April, May, of June, and July-flowers;
I sing of May-poles, hock-carts, wassails, wakes,
Of bride-grooms, brides, and of their bridal-cakes.
I write of Youth, of Love;--and have access
By these, to sing of cleanly wantonness;
I sing of dews, of rains, and, piece by piece,
Of balm, of oil, of spice, and ambergris.
I sing of times trans-shifting; and I write
How roses first came red, and lilies white.
I write of groves, of twilights, and I sing
The court of Mab, and of the Fairy King.
I write of Hell; I sing, and ever shall
Of Heaven,--and hope to have it after all.

2

TO HIS MUSE

Whither, mad maiden, wilt thou roam?
Far safer 'twere to stay at home;
Where thou mayst sit, and piping, please
The poor and private cottages.
Since cotes and hamlets best agree
With this thy meaner minstrelsy.
There with the reed thou mayst express
The shepherd's fleecy happiness;
And with thy Eclogues intermix:
Some smooth and harmless Bucolics.
There, on a hillock, thou mayst sing
Unto a handsome shepherdling;
Or to a girl, that keeps the neat,
With breath more sweet than violet.
There, there, perhaps such lines as these
May take the simple villages;
But for the court, the country wit
Is despicable unto it.
Stay then at home, and do not go
Or fly abroad to seek for woe;
Contempts in courts and cities dwell
No critic haunts the poor man's cell,
Where thou mayst hear thine own lines read
By no one tongue there censured.
That man's unwise will search for ill,
And may prevent it, sitting still.

3

WHEN HE WOULD HAVE HIS VERSES READ

In sober mornings, do not thou rehearse
The holy incantation of a verse;
But when that men have both well drunk, and fed,
Let my enchantments then be sung or read.
When laurel spirts i' th' fire, and when the hearth
Smiles to itself, and gilds the roof with mirth;
When up the Thyrse is raised, and when the sound
Of sacred orgies, flies A round, A round;
When the rose reigns, and locks with ointments shine,
Let rigid Cato read these lines of mine.

4

TO HIS BOOK

Make haste away, and let one be
A friendly patron unto thee;
Lest, rapt from hence, I see thee lie
Torn for the use of pastery;
Or see thy injured leaves serve well
To make loose gowns for mackarel;
Or see the grocers, in a trice,
Make hoods of thee to serve out spice.

5

TO HIS BOOK

Take mine advice, and go not near
Those faces, sour as vinegar;
For these, and nobler numbers, can
Ne'er please the supercilious man.

6

TO HIS BOOK

Be bold, my Book, nor be abash'd, or fear
The cutting thumb-nail, or the brow severe;
But by the Muses swear, all here is good,
If but well read, or ill read, understood.

7

TO MISTRESS KATHARINE BRADSHAW, THE LOVELY,
THAT CROWNED HIM WITH LAUREL

My Muse in meads has spent her many hours
Sitting, and sorting several sorts of flowers,
To make for others garlands; and to set
On many a head here, many a coronet.
But amongst all encircled here, not one
Gave her a day of coronation;
Till you, sweet mistress, came and interwove
A laurel for her, ever young as Love.
You first of all crown'd her; she must, of due,
Render for that, a crown of life to you.

8

TO HIS VERSES

What will ye, my poor orphans, do,
When I must leave the world and you;
Who'll give ye then a sheltering shed,
Or credit ye, when I am dead?
Who'll let ye by their fire sit,
Although ye have a stock of wit,
Already coin'd to pay for it?
--I cannot tell: unless there be
Some race of old humanity
Left, of the large heart and long hand,
Alive, as noble Westmorland;
Or gallant Newark; which brave two
May fost'ring fathers be to you.
If not, expect to be no less
Ill used, than babes left fatherless.

9

NOT EVERY DAY FIT FOR VERSE

'Tis not ev'ry day that I
Fitted am to prophesy:
No, but when the spirit fills
The fantastic pannicles,
Full of fire, then I write
As the Godhead doth indite.
Thus enraged, my lines are hurl'd,
Like the Sibyl's, through the world:

Look how next the holy fire
Either slakes, or doth retire;
So the fancy cools:--till when
That brave spirit comes again.

10

HIS PRAYER TO BEN JONSON

When I a verse shall make,
Know I have pray'd thee,
For old religion's sake,
Saint Ben, to aid me

Make the way smooth for me,
When, I, thy Herrick,
Honouring thee on my knee
Offer my Lyric.

Candles I'll give to thee,
And a new altar;
And thou, Saint Ben, shalt be
Writ in my psalter.

11

HIS REQUEST TO JULIA

Julia, if I chance to die
Ere I print my poetry,
I most humbly thee desire

To commit it to the fire:
Better 'twere my book were dead,
Than to live not perfected.

12

TO HIS BOOK

Go thou forth, my book, though late,
Yet be timely fortunate.
It may chance good luck may send
Thee a kinsman or a friend,
That may harbour thee, when I
With my fates neglected lie.
If thou know'st not where to dwell,
See, the fire's by.--Farewell!

13

HIS POETRY HIS PILLAR

Only a little more
I have to write:
Then I'll give o'er,
And bid the world good-night.

'Tis but a flying minute,
That I must stay,
Or linger in it:
And then I must away.

O Time, that cut'st down all,
And scarce leav'st here
Memorial
Of any men that were;

--How many lie forgot
In vaults beneath,
And piece-meal rot
Without a fame in death?

Behold this living stone
I rear for me,
Ne'er to be thrown
Down, envious Time, by thee.

Pillars let some set up
If so they please;
Here is my hope,
And my Pyramides.

14

TO HIS BOOK

If hap it must, that I must see thee lie
Absyrtus-like, all torn confusedly;
With solemn tears, and with much grief of heart,
I'll recollect thee, weeping, part by part;
And having wash'd thee, close thee in a chest
With spice; that done, I'll leave thee to thy rest.

15

UPON HIMSELF

Thou shalt not all die; for while Love's fire shines
Upon his altar, men shall read thy lines;
And learn'd musicians shall, to honour Herrick's
Fame, and his name, both set and sing his lyrics.

To his book's end this last line he'd have placed:--
Jocund his Muse was, but his Life was chaste.

** IDYLLICA **

16

THE COUNTRY LIFE:

TO THE HONOURED MR ENDYMION PORTER, GROOM OF
THE BED-CHAMBER TO HIS MAJESTY

Sweet country life, to such unknown,
Whose lives are others', not their own!
But serving courts and cities, be
Less happy, less enjoying thee.
Thou never plough'st the ocean's foam
To seek and bring rough pepper home:
Nor to the Eastern Ind dost rove
To bring from thence the scorched clove:
Nor, with the loss of thy loved rest,
Bring'st home the ingot from the West.

No, thy ambition's master-piece
Flies no thought higher than a fleece:
Or how to pay thy hinds, and clear
All scores: and so to end the year:
But walk'st about thine own dear bounds,
Not envying others' larger grounds:
For well thou know'st, 'tis not th' extent
Of land makes life, but sweet content.
When now the cock (the ploughman's horn)
Calls forth the lily-wristed morn;
Then to thy corn-fields thou dost go,
Which though well soil'd, yet thou dost know
That the best compost for the lands
Is the wise master's feet, and hands.
There at the plough thou find'st thy team,
With a hind whistling there to them:
And cheer'st them up, by singing how
The kingdom's portion is the plough.
This done, then to th' enamell'd meads
Thou go'st; and as thy foot there treads,
Thou seest a present God-like power
Imprinted in each herb and flower:
And smell'st the breath of great-eyed kine,
Sweet as the blossoms of the vine.
Here thou behold'st thy large sleek neat
Unto the dew-laps up in meat:
And, as thou look'st, the wanton steer,
The heifer, cow, and ox draw near,
To make a pleasing pastime there.
These seen, thou go'st to view thy flocks
Of sheep, safe from the wolf and fox,
And find'st their bellies there as full
Of short sweet grass, as backs with wool:

And leav'st them, as they feed and fill,
A shepherd piping on a hill.

For sports, for pageantry, and plays,
Thou hast thy eves, and holydays:
On which the young men and maids meet,
To exercise their dancing feet:
Tripping the comely country Round,
With daffadils and daisies crown'd.
Thy wakes, thy quintels, here thou hast,
Thy May-poles too with garlands graced;
Thy Morris-dance; thy Whitsun-ale;
Thy shearing-feast, which never fail.
Thy harvest home; thy wassail bowl,
That's toss'd up after Fox i' th' hole:
Thy mummeries; thy Twelve-tide kings
And queens; thy Christmas revellings:
Thy nut-brown mirth, thy russet wit,
And no man pays too dear for it.--
To these, thou hast thy times to go
And trace the hare i' th' treacherous snow:
Thy witty wiles to draw, and get
The lark into the trammel net:
Thou hast thy cockrood, and thy glade
To take the precious pheasant made:
Thy lime-twigs, snares, and pit-falls then
To catch the pilfering birds, not men.

--O happy life! if that their good
The husbandmen but understood!
Who all the day themselves do please,
And younglings, with such sports as these:
And lying down, have nought t' affright

Sweet Sleep, that makes more short the night.
CAETERA DESUNT--

17

TO PHILLIS, TO LOVE AND LIVE WITH HIM

Live, live with me, and thou shalt see
The pleasures I'll prepare for thee:
What sweets the country can afford
Shall bless thy bed, and bless thy board.
The soft sweet moss shall be thy bed,
With crawling woodbine over-spread:
By which the silver-shedding streams
Shall gently melt thee into dreams.
Thy clothing next, shall be a gown
Made of the fleeces' purest down.
The tongues of kids shall be thy meat;
Their milk thy drink; and thou shalt eat
The paste of filberts for thy bread
With cream of cowslips buttered:
Thy feasting-table shall be hills
With daisies spread, and daffadils;
Where thou shalt sit, and Red-breast by,
For meat, shall give thee melody.
I'll give thee chains and carcanets
Of primroses and violets.
A bag and bottle thou shalt have,
That richly wrought, and this as brave;
So that as either shall express
The wearer's no mean shepherdess.
At shearing-times, and yearly wakes,

When Themilis his pastime makes,
There thou shalt be; and be the wit,
Nay more, the feast, and grace of it.
On holydays, when virgins meet
To dance the heys with nimble feet,
Thou shalt come forth, and then appear
The Queen of Roses for that year.
And having danced ('bove all the best)
Carry the garland from the rest,
In wicker-baskets maids shall bring
To thee, my dearest shepherdling,
The blushing apple, bashful pear,
And shame-faced plum, all simp'ring there.
Walk in the groves, and thou shalt find
The name of Phillis in the rind
Of every straight and smooth-skin tree;
Where kissing that, I'll twice kiss thee.
To thee a sheep-hook I will send,
Be-prank'd with ribbands, to this end,
This, this alluring hook might be
Less for to catch a sheep, than me.
Thou shalt have possets, wassails fine,
Not made of ale, but spiced wine;
To make thy maids and self free mirth,
All sitting near the glitt'ring hearth.
Thou shalt have ribbands, roses, rings,
Gloves, garters, stockings, shoes, and strings
Of winning colours, that shall move
Others to lust, but me to love.
--These, nay, and more, thine own shall be,
If thou wilt love, and live with me.

18

THE WASSAIL

Give way, give way, ye gates, and win
An easy blessing to your bin
And basket, by our entering in.

May both with manchet stand replete;
Your larders, too, so hung with meat,
That though a thousand, thousand eat,

Yet, ere twelve moons shall whirl about
Their silv'ry spheres, there's none may doubt
But more's sent in than was served out.

Next, may your dairies prosper so,
As that your pans no ebb may know;
But if they do, the more to flow,

Like to a solemn sober stream,
Bank'd all with lilies, and the cream
Of sweetest cowslips filling them.

Then may your plants be press'd with fruit,
Nor bee or hive you have be mute,
But sweetly sounding like a lute.

Last, may your harrows, shares, and ploughs,
Your stacks, your stocks, your sweetest mows,
All prosper by your virgin-vows.

--Alas! we bless, but see none here,

That brings us either ale or beer;
In a dry-house all things are near.

Let's leave a longer time to wait,
Where rust and cobwebs bind the gate;
And all live here with needy fate;

Where chimneys do for ever weep
For want of warmth, and stomachs keep
With noise the servants' eyes from sleep.

It is in vain to sing, or stay
Our free feet here, but we'll away:
Yet to the Lares this we'll say:

'The time will come when you'll be sad,
'And reckon this for fortune bad,
'T'ave lost the good ye might have had.'

19

THE FAIRIES

If ye will with Mab find grace,
Set each platter in his place;
Rake the fire up, and get
Water in, ere sun be set.
Wash your pails and cleanse your dairies,
Sluts are loathsome to the fairies;
Sweep your house; Who doth not so,
Mab will pinch her by the toe.

20

CEREMONY UPON CANDLEMAS EVE

Down with the rosemary, and so
Down with the bays and misletoe;
Down with the holly, ivy, all
Wherewith ye dress'd the Christmas hall;
That so the superstitious find
No one least branch there left behind;
For look, how many leaves there be
Neglected there, maids, trust to me,
So many goblins you shall see.

21

CEREMONIES FOR CANDLEMAS EVE

Down with the rosemary and bays,
Down with the misletoe;
Instead of holly, now up-raise
The greener box, for show.

The holly hitherto did sway;
Let box now domineer,
Until the dancing Easter-day,
Or Easter's eve appear.

Then youthful box, which now hath grace
Your houses to renew,
Grown old, surrender must his place

Unto the crisped yew.

When yew is out, then birch comes in,
And many flowers beside,
Both of a fresh and fragrant kin,
To honour Whitsuntide.

Green rushes then, and sweetest bents,
With cooler oaken boughs,
Come in for comely ornaments,
To re-adorn the house.
Thus times do shift; each thing his turn does hold;
New things succeed, as former things grow old.

22

THE CEREMONIES FOR CANDLEMAS DAY

Kindle the Christmas brand, and then
Till sunset let it burn;
Which quench'd, then lay it up again,
Till Christmas next return.

Part must be kept, wherewith to teend
The Christmas log next year;
And where 'tis safely kept, the fiend
Can do no mischief there.

23

FAREWELL FROST, OR WELCOME SPRING

Fled are the frosts, and now the fields appear
Reclothed in fresh and verdant diaper;
Thaw'd are the snows; and now the lusty Spring
Gives to each mead a neat enamelling;
The palms put forth their gems, and every tree
Now swaggers in her leafy gallantry.
The while the Daulian minstrel sweetly sings
With warbling notes her Terean sufferings.
--What gentle winds perspire! as if here
Never had been the northern plunderer
To strip the trees and fields, to their distress,
Leaving them to a pitied nakedness.
And look how when a frantic storm doth tear
A stubborn oak or holm, long growing there,--
But lull'd to calmness, then succeeds a breeze
That scarcely stirs the nodding leaves of trees;
So when this war, which tempest-like doth spoil
Our salt, our corn, our honey, wine, and oil,
Falls to a temper, and doth mildly cast
His inconsiderate frenzy off, at last,
The gentle dove may, when these turmoils cease,
Bring in her bill, once more, the branch of Peace.

24

TO THE MAIDS, TO WALK ABROAD

Come, sit we under yonder tree,
Where merry as the maids we'll be;
And as on primroses we sit,
We'll venture, if we can, at wit;

If not, at draw-gloves we will play,
So spend some minutes of the day;
Or else spin out the thread of sands,
Playing at questions and commands:
Or tell what strange tricks Love can do,
By quickly making one of two.
Thus we will sit and talk, but tell
No cruel truths of Philomel,
Or Phillis, whom hard fate forced on
To kill herself for Demophon;
But fables we'll relate; how Jove
Put on all shapes to get a Love;
As now a satyr, then a swan,
A bull but then, and now a man.
Next, we will act how young men woo,
And sigh and kiss as lovers do;
And talk of brides; and who shall make
That wedding-smock, this bridal-cake,
That dress, this sprig, that leaf, this vine,
That smooth and silken columbine.
This done, we'll draw lots who shall buy
And gild the bays and rosemary;
What posies for our wedding rings;
What gloves we'll give, and ribbonings;
And smiling at our selves, decree
Who then the joining priest shall be;
What short sweet prayers shall be said,
And how the posset shall be made
With cream of lilies, not of kine,
And maiden's-blush for spiced wine.
Thus having talk'd, we'll next commend
A kiss to each, and so we'll end.

25

CORINA'S GOING A MAYING

Get up, get up for shame! the blooming morn
Upon her wings presents the god unshorn.
See how Aurora throws her fair
Fresh-quilted colours through the air:
Get up, sweet-slug-a-bed, and see
The dew bespangling herb and tree.
Each flower has wept, and bow'd toward the east,
Above an hour since; yet you not drest,
Nay! not so much as out of bed?
When all the birds have matins said,
And sung their thankful hymns: 'tis sin,
Nay, profanation, to keep in,--
Whenas a thousand virgins on this day,
Spring, sooner than the lark, to fetch in May.

Rise; and put on your foliage, and be seen
To come forth, like the Spring-time, fresh and green,
And sweet as Flora. Take no care
For jewels for your gown, or hair:
Fear not; the leaves will strew
Gems in abundance upon you:
Besides, the childhood of the day has kept,
Against you come, some orient pearls unwept:
Come, and receive them while the light
Hangs on the dew-locks of the night:
And Titan on the eastern hill
Retires himself, or else stands still
Till you come forth. Wash, dress, be brief in praying:

Few beads are best, when once we go a Maying.

Come, my Corinna, come; and coming, mark
How each field turns a street; each street a park
Made green, and trimm'd with trees: see how
Devotion gives each house a bough
Or branch: each porch, each door, ere this,
An ark, a tabernacle is
Made up of white-thorn neatly interwove;
As if here were those cooler shades of love.
Can such delights be in the street,
And open fields, and we not see't?
Come, we'll abroad: and let's obey
The proclamation made for May:
And sin no more, as we have done, by staying;
But, my Corinna, come, let's go a Maying.

There's not a budding boy, or girl, this day,
But is got up, and gone to bring in May.
A deal of youth, ere this, is come
Back, and with white-thorn laden home.
Some have dispatch'd their cakes and cream,
Before that we have left to dream:
And some have wept, and woo'd, and plighted troth,
And chose their priest, ere we can cast off sloth:
Many a green-gown has been given;
Many a kiss, both odd and even:
Many a glance, too, has been sent
From out the eye, love's firmament:
Many a jest told of the keys betraying
This night, and locks pick'd:--yet we're not a Maying.

--Come, let us go, while we are in our prime;

And take the harmless folly of the time!
We shall grow old apace, and die
Before we know our liberty.
Our life is short; and our days run
As fast away as does the sun:--
And as a vapour, or a drop of rain
Once lost, can ne'er be found again:
So when or you or I are made
A fable, song, or fleeting shade;
All love, all liking, all delight
Lies drown'd with us in endless night.
--Then while time serves, and we are but decaying,
Come, my Corinna! come, let's go a Maying.

26

THE MAYPOLE

The May-pole is up,
Now give me the cup;
I'll drink to the garlands around it;
But first unto those
Whose hands did compose
The glory of flowers that crown'd it.

A health to my girls,
Whose husbands may earls
Or lords be, granting my wishes,
And when that ye wed
To the bridal bed,
Then multiply all, like to fishes.

27

THE WAKE

Come, Anthea, let us two
Go to feast, as others do:
Tarts and custards, creams and cakes,
Are the junkets still at wakes;
Unto which the tribes resort,
Where the business is the sport:
Morris-dancers thou shalt see,
Marian, too, in pageantry;
And a mimic to devise
Many grinning properties.
Players there will be, and those
Base in action as in clothes;
Yet with strutting they will please
The incurious villages.
Near the dying of the day
There will be a cudgel-play,
Where a coxcomb will be broke,
Ere a good word can be spoke:
But the anger ends all here,
Drench'd in ale, or drown'd in beer.
--Happy rusticks! best content
With the cheapest merriment;
And possess no other fear,
Than to want the Wake next year.

28

THE HOCK-CART, OR HARVEST HOME:
TO THE RIGHT HONOURABLE MILDMAY, EARL OF WESTMORLAND

Come, Sons of Summer, by whose toil
We are the lords of wine and oil:
By whose tough labours, and rough hands,
We rip up first, then reap our lands.
Crown'd with the ears of corn, now come,
And, to the pipe, sing Harvest Home.

Come forth, my lord, and see the cart
Drest up with all the country art.
See, here a maukin, there a sheet,
As spotless pure, as it is sweet:
The horses, mares, and frisking fillies,
Clad, all, in linen white as lilies.
The harvest swains and wenches bound
For joy, to see the Hock-Cart crown'd.
About the cart, hear, how the rout
Of rural younglings raise the shout;
Pressing before, some coming after,
Those with a shout, and these with laughter.
Some bless the cart; some kiss the sheaves;
Some prank them up with oaken leaves:
Some cross the fill-horse; some with great
Devotion, stroke the home-borne wheat:
While other rustics, less attent
To prayers, than to merriment,
Run after with their breeches rent.
--Well, on, brave boys, to your lord's hearth,
Glitt'ring with fire; where, for your mirth,
Ye shall see first the large and chief
Foundation of your feast, fat beef;

With upper stories, mutton, veal
And bacon, which makes full the meal,
With sev'ral dishes standing by,
As here a custard, there a pie,
And here, all tempting frumenty.
And for to make the merry cheer,
If smirking wine be wanting here,
There's that which drowns all care, stout beer:
Which freely drink to your lord's health
Then to the plough, the common-wealth;
Next to your flails, your fanes, your vats;
Then to the maids with wheaten hats:
To the rough sickle, and crookt scythe,--
Drink, frolic, boys, till all be blythe.
Feed, and grow fat; and as ye eat,
Be mindful, that the lab'ring neat,
As you, may have their fill of meat.
And know, besides, ye must revoke
The patient ox unto the yoke,
And all go back unto the plough
And harrow, though they're hang'd up now.
And, you must know, your lord's word's true,
Feed him ye must, whose food fills you;
And that this pleasure is like rain,
Not sent ye for to drown your pain,
But for to make it spring again.

29

THE BRIDE-CAKE

This day, my Julia, thou must make

For Mistress Bride the wedding-cake:
Knead but the dough, and it will be
To paste of almonds turn'd by thee;
Or kiss it thou but once or twice,
And for the bride-cake there'll be spice.

30

THE OLD WIVES' PRAYER

Holy-Rood, come forth and shield
Us i' th' city and the field;
Safely guard us, now and aye,
From the blast that burns by day;
And those sounds that us affright
In the dead of dampish night;
Drive all hurtful fiends us fro,
By the time the cocks first crow.

31

THE BELL-MAN

From noise of scare-fires rest ye free
From murders, Benedicite;
From all mischances that may fright
Your pleasing slumbers in the night
Mercy secure ye all, and keep
The goblin from ye, while ye sleep.
--Past one a clock, and almost two,--
My masters all, 'Good day to you.'

33

TO THE GENIUS OF HIS HOUSE

Command the roof, great Genius, and from thence
Into this house pour down thy influence,
That through each room a golden pipe may run
Of living water by thy benizon;
Fulfil the larders, and with strength'ning bread
Be ever-more these bins replenished.
Next, like a bishop consecrate my ground,
That lucky fairies here may dance their round;
And, after that, lay down some silver pence,
The master's charge and care to recompence.
Charm then the chambers; make the beds for ease,
More than for peevish pining sicknesses;
Fix the foundation fast, and let the roof
Grow old with time, but yet keep weather-proof.

33

HIS GRANGE, OR PRIVATE WEALTH

Though clock,
To tell how night draws hence, I've none,
A cock
I have to sing how day draws on:
I have
A maid, my Prue, by good luck sent,
To save

That little, Fates me gave or lent.
A hen
I keep, which, creeking day by day,
Tells when
She goes her long white egg to lay:
A goose
I have, which, with a jealous ear,
Lets loose
Her tongue, to tell what danger's near.
A lamb
I keep, tame, with my morsels fed,
Whose dam
An orphan left him, lately dead:
A cat
I keep, that plays about my house,
Grown fat
With eating many a miching mouse:
To these
A Trasy I do keep, whereby
I please
The more my rural privacy:
Which are
But toys, to give my heart some ease:--
Where care
None is, slight things do lightly please.

34

A PASTORAL UPON THE BIRTH OF PRINCE CHARLES:
PRESENTED TO THE KING, AND SET BY MR NIC. LANIERE

THE SPEAKERS: MIRTILLO, AMINTAS, AND AMARILLIS

AMIN. Good day, Mirtillo. MIRT. And to you no less;
And all fair signs lead on our shepherdess.
AMAR. With all white luck to you. MIRT. But say,
What news
Stirs in our sheep-walk? AMIN. None, save that my
ewes,
My wethers, lambs, and wanton kids are well,
Smooth, fair, and fat; none better I can tell:
Or that this day Menalchas keeps a feast
For his sheep-shearers. MIRT. True, these are the least.
But dear Amintas, and sweet Amarillis,
Rest but a while here by this bank of lilies;
And lend a gentle ear to one report
The country has. AMIN. From whence? AMAR. From
whence? MIRT. The Court.
Three days before the shutting-in of May,
(With whitest wool be ever crown'd that day!)
To all our joy, a sweet-faced child was born,
More tender than the childhood of the morn.
CHORUS:--Pan pipe to him, and bleats of lambs and
sheep
Let lullaby the pretty prince asleep!
MIRT. And that his birth should be more singular,
At noon of day was seen a silver star,
Bright as the wise men's torch, which guided them
To God's sweet babe, when born at Bethlehem;
While golden angels, some have told to me,
Sung out his birth with heav'nly minstrelsy.
AMIN. O rare! But is't a trespass, if we three
Should wend along his baby-ship to see?
MIRT. Not so, not so. CHOR. But if it chance to prove
At most a fault, 'tis but a fault of love.

AMAR. But, dear Mirtillo, I have heard it told,
Those learned men brought incense, myrrh, and gold,
From countries far, with store of spices sweet,
And laid them down for offerings at his feet.
MIRT. 'Tis true, indeed; and each of us will bring
Unto our smiling and our blooming King,
A neat, though not so great an offering.
AMAR. A garland for my gift shall be,
Of flowers ne'er suck'd by th' thieving bee;
And all most sweet, yet all less sweet than he.
AMIN. And I will bear along with you
Leaves dropping down the honied dew,
With oaten pipes, as sweet, as new.
MIRT. And I a sheep-hook will bestow
To have his little King-ship know,
As he is Prince, he's Shepherd too.
CHOR. Come, let's away, and quickly let's be drest,
And quickly give:--the swiftest grace is best.
And when before him we have laid our treasures,
We'll bless the babe:--then back to country pleasures.

35

A DIALOGUE BETWIXT HIMSELF AND MISTRESS ELIZA
WHEELER, UNDER THE NAME OF AMARILLIS

My dearest Love, since thou wilt go,
And leave me here behind thee;
For love or pity, let me know
The place where I may find thee.

AMARIL. In country meadows, pearl'd with dew,

And set about with lilies;
There, filling maunds with cowslips, you
May find your Amarillis.

HER. What have the meads to do with thee,
Or with thy youthful hours?
Live thou at court, where thou mayst be
The queen of men, not flowers.

Let country wenches make 'em fine
With posies, since 'tis fitter
For thee with richest gems to shine,
And like the stars to glitter.

AMARIL. You set too-high a rate upon
A shepherdess so homely.
HER. Believe it, dearest, there's not one
I' th' court that's half so comely.

I prithee stay. AMARIL. I must away;
Let's kiss first, then we'll sever;
AMBO And though we bid adieu to day,
We shall not part for ever.

36

A BUCOLIC BETWIXT TWO;
LACON AND THYRSIS

LACON. For a kiss or two, confess,
What doth cause this pensiveness,
Thou most lovely neat-herdess?

Why so lonely on the hill?
Why thy pipe by thee so still,
That erewhile was heard so shrill?
Tell me, do thy kine now fail
To fulfil the milking-pail?
Say, what is't that thou dost ail?

THYR. None of these; but out, alas!
A mischance is come to pass,
And I'll tell thee what it was:
See, mine eyes are weeping ripe.
LACON. Tell, and I'll lay down my pipe.

THYR. I have lost my lovely steer,
That to me was far more dear
Than these kine which I milk here;
Broad of forehead, large of eye,
Party-colour'd like a pye,
Smooth in each limb as a die;
Clear of hoof, and clear of horn,
Sharply pointed as a thorn;
With a neck by yoke unworn,
From the which hung down by strings,
Balls of cowslips, daisy rings,
Interplaced with ribbonings;
Faultless every way for shape;
Not a straw could him escape,
Ever gamesome as an ape,
But yet harmless as a sheep.
Pardon, Lacon, if I weep;
Tears will spring where woes are deep.
Now, ai me! ai me! Last night
Came a mad dog, and did bite,

Ay, and kill'd my dear delight.

LACON Alack, for grief!
THYR. But I'll be brief.
Hence I must, for time doth call
Me, and my sad playmates all,
To his evening funeral.
Live long, Lacon; so adieu!

LACON Mournful maid, farewell to you;
Earth afford ye flowers to strew!

37

A PASTORAL SUNG TO THE KING

MONTANO, SILVIO, AND MIRTILLO, SHEPHERDS

MON. Bad are the times. SIL. And worse than they are we.
MON. Troth, bad are both; worse fruit, and ill the tree:
The feast of shepherds fail. SIL. None crowns the cup
Of wassail now, or sets the quintel up:
And he, who used to lead the country-round,
Youthful Mirtillo, here he comes, grief-drown'd.
AMBO. Let's cheer him up. SIL. Behold him weeping-ripe.
MIRT. Ah, Amarillis! farewell mirth and pipe;
Since thou art gone, no more I mean to play
To these smooth lawns, my mirthful roundelay.
Dear Amarillis! MON. Hark! SIL. Mark! MIRT. This earth grew sweet
Where, Amarillis, thou didst set thy feet.
AMBO Poor pitied youth! MIRT. And here the breath

of kine
And sheep grew more sweet by that breath of thine.
This dock of wool, and this rich lock of hair,
This ball of cowslips, these she gave me here.
SIL. Words sweet as love itself. MON. Hark!--
MIRT. This way she came, and this way too she went;
How each thing smells divinely redolent!
Like to a field of beans, when newly blown,
Or like a meadow being lately mown.
MON. A sweet sad passion----
MIRT. In dewy mornings, when she came this way,
Sweet bents would bow, to give my Love the day;
And when at night she folded had her sheep,
Daisies would shut, and closing, sigh and weep.
Besides (Ai me!) since she went hence to dwell,
The Voice's Daughter ne'er spake syllable.
But she is gone. SIL. Mirtillo, tell us whither?
MIRT. Where she and I shall never meet together.
MON. Fore-fend it, Pan! and Pales, do thou please
To give an end... MIRT. To what? SIL. Such griefs as these.
MIRT. Never, O never! Still I may endure
The wound I suffer, never find a cure.
MON. Love, for thy sake, will bring her to these hills
And dales again. MIRT. No, I will languish still;
And all the while my part shall be to weep;
And with my sighs call home my bleating sheep;
And in the rind of every comely tree
I'll carve thy name, and in that name kiss thee.
MON. Set with the sun, thy woes! SIL. The day grows old;
And time it is our full-fed flocks to fold.
CHOR. The shades grow great; but greater grows

our sorrow:--
But let's go steep
Our eyes in sleep;
And meet to weep
To-morrow.

38

TO THE WILLOW-TREE

Thou art to all lost love the best,
The only true plant found,
Wherewith young men and maids distrest
And left of love, are crown'd.

When once the lover's rose is dead
Or laid aside forlorn,
Then willow-garlands, 'bout the head,
Bedew'd with tears, are worn.

When with neglect, the lover's bane,
Poor maids rewarded be,
For their love lost their only gain
Is but a wreath from thee.

And underneath thy cooling shade,
When weary of the light,
The love-spent youth, and love-sick maid,
Come to weep out the night.

39

THE FAIRY TEMPLE; OR, OBERON'S CHAPEL

DEDICATED TO MR JOHN MERRIFIELD, COUNSELLOR AT LAW

RARE TEMPLES THOU HAST SEEN, I KNOW,
AND RICH FOR IN AND OUTWARD SHOW;
SURVEY THIS CHAPEL BUILT, ALONE,
WITHOUT OR LIME, OR WOOD, OR STONE.
THEN SAY, IF ONE THOU'ST SEEN MORE FINE
THAN THIS, THE FAIRIES' ONCE, NOW THINE.

THE TEMPLE

A way enchaced with glass and beads
There is, that to the Chapel leads;
Whose structure, for his holy rest,
Is here the Halcyon's curious nest;
Into the which who looks, shall see
His Temple of Idolatry;
Where he of god-heads has such store,
As Rome's Pantheon had not more.
His house of Rimmon this he calls,
Girt with small bones, instead of walls.
First in a niche, more black than jet,
His idol-cricket there is set;
Then in a polish'd oval by
There stands his idol-beetle-fly;
Next, in an arch, akin to this,
His idol-canker seated is.
Then in a round, is placed by these
His golden god, Cantharides.

So that where'er ye look, ye see
No capital, no cornice free,
Or frieze, from this fine frippery.
Now this the Fairies would have known,
Theirs is a mixt religion:
And some have heard the elves it call
Part Pagan, part Papistical.
If unto me all tongues were granted,
I could not speak the saints here painted.
Saint Tit, Saint Nit, Saint Is, Saint Itis,
Who 'gainst Mab's state placed here right is.
Saint Will o' th' Wisp, of no great bigness,
But, alias, call'd here FATUUS IGNIS.
Saint Frip, Saint Trip, Saint Fill, Saint Filly;--
Neither those other saint-ships will I
Here go about for to recite
Their number, almost infinite;
Which, one by one, here set down are
In this most curious calendar.

First, at the entrance of the gate,
A little puppet-priest doth wait,
Who squeaks to all the comers there,
'Favour your tongues, who enter here.
'Pure hands bring hither, without stain.'
A second pules, 'Hence, hence, profane!'
Hard by, i' th' shell of half a nut,
The holy-water there is put;
A little brush of squirrels' hairs,
Composed of odd, not even pairs,
Stands in the platter, or close by,
To purge the fairy family.
Near to the altar stands the priest,

There offering up the holy-grist;
Ducking in mood and perfect tense,
With (much good do't him) reverence.
The altar is not here four-square,
Nor in a form triangular;
Nor made of glass, or wood, or stone,
But of a little transverse bone;
Which boys and bruckel'd children call
(Playing for points and pins) cockall.
Whose linen-drapery is a thin,
Subtile, and ductile codling's skin;
Which o'er the board is smoothly spread
With little seal-work damasked.
The fringe that circumbinds it, too,
Is spangle-work of trembling dew,
Which, gently gleaming, makes a show,
Like frost-work glitt'ring on the snow.
Upon this fetuous board doth stand
Something for shew-bread, and at hand
(Just in the middle of the altar)
Upon an end, the Fairy-psalter,
Graced with the trout-flies' curious wings,
Which serve for watchet ribbonings.
Now, we must know, the elves are led
Right by the Rubric, which they read:
And if report of them be true,
They have their text for what they do;
Ay, and their book of canons too.
And, as Sir Thomas Parson tells,
They have their book of articles;
And if that Fairy knight not lies
They have their book of homilies;
And other Scriptures, that design

A short, but righteous discipline.
The bason stands the board upon
To take the free-oblation;
A little pin-dust, which they hold
More precious than we prize our gold;
Which charity they give to many
Poor of the parish, if there's any.
Upon the ends of these neat rails,
Hatch'd with the silver-light of snails,
The elves, in formal manner, fix
Two pure and holy candlesticks,
In either which a tall small bent
Burns for the altar's ornament.
For sanctity, they have, to these,
Their curious copes and surplices
Of cleanest cobweb, hanging by
In their religious vestery.
They have their ash-pans and their brooms,
To purge the chapel and the rooms;
Their many mumbling mass-priests here,
And many a dapper chorister.
Their ush'ring vergers here likewise,
Their canons and their chaunteries;
Of cloister-monks they have enow,
Ay, and their abbey-lubbers too:--
And if their legend do not lie,
They much affect the papacy;
And since the last is dead, there's hope
Elve Boniface shall next be Pope.
They have their cups and chalices,
Their pardons and indulgences,
Their beads of nits, bells, books, and wax-
Candles, forsooth, and other knacks;

Their holy oil, their fasting-spittle,
Their sacred salt here, not a little.
Dry chips, old shoes, rags, grease, and bones,
Beside their fumigations.
Many a trifle, too, and trinket,
And for what use, scarce man would think it.
Next then, upon the chanter's side
An apple's-core is hung up dried,
With rattling kernels, which is rung
To call to morn and even-song.
The saint, to which the most he prays
And offers incense nights and days,
The lady of the lobster is,
Whose foot-pace he doth stroke and kiss,
And, humbly, chives of saffron brings
For his most cheerful offerings.
When, after these, he's paid his vows,
He lowly to the altar bows;
And then he dons the silk-worm's shed,
Like a Turk's turban on his head,
And reverently departeth thence,
Hid in a cloud of frankincense;
And by the glow-worm's light well guided,
Goes to the Feast that's now provided.

40

OBERON'S FEAST

SHAPCOT! TO THE THE FAIRY STATE
I WITH DISCRETION DEDICATE:
BECAUSE THOU PRIZEST THINGS THAT ARE

CURIOUS AND UNFAMILIAR.
TAKE FIRST THE FEAST; THESE DISHES GONE,
WE'LL SEE THE FAIRY COURT ANON.

A little mushroom-table spread,
After short prayers, they set on bread,
A moon-parch'd grain of purest wheat,
With some small glitt'ring grit, to eat
His choice bits with; then in a trice
They make a feast less great than nice.
But all this while his eye is served,
We must not think his ear was sterved;
But that there was in place to stir
His spleen, the chirring grasshopper,
The merry cricket, puling fly,
The piping gnat for minstrelsy.
And now, we must imagine first,
The elves present, to quench his thirst,
A pure seed-pearl of infant dew,
Brought and besweeten'd in a blue
And pregnant violet; which done,
His kitling eyes begin to run
Quite through the table, where he spies
The horns of papery butterflies,
Of which he eats; and tastes a little
Of that we call the cuckoo's spittle;
A little fuz-ball pudding stands
By, yet not blessed by his hands,
That was too coarse; but then forthwith
He ventures boldly on the pith
Of sugar'd rush, and eats the sagge
And well-bestrutted bees' sweet bag;
Gladding his palate with some store

Of emmets' eggs; what would he more?
But beards of mice, a newt's stew'd thigh,
A bloated earwig, and a fly;
With the red-capt worm, that's shut
Within the concave of a nut,
Brown as his tooth. A little moth,
Late fatten'd in a piece of cloth;
With wither'd cherries, mandrakes' ears,
Moles' eyes: to these the slain stag's tears;
The unctuous dewlaps of a snail,
The broke-heart of a nightingale
O'ercome in music; with a wine
Ne'er ravish'd from the flattering vine,
But gently prest from the soft side
Of the most sweet and dainty bride,
Brought in a dainty daisy, which
He fully quaffs up, to bewitch
His blood to height; this done, commended
Grace by his priest; The feast is ended.

41

THE BEGGAR TO MAB, THE FAIRY QUEEN

Please your Grace, from out your store
Give an alms to one that's poor,
That your mickle may have more.
Black I'm grown for want of meat,
Give me then an ant to eat,
Or the cleft ear of a mouse
Over-sour'd in drink of souce;
Or, sweet lady, reach to me

The abdomen of a bee;
Or commend a cricket's hip,
Or his huckson, to my scrip;
Give for bread, a little bit
Of a pease that 'gins to chit,
And my full thanks take for it.
Flour of fuz-balls, that's too good
For a man in needy-hood;
But the meal of mill-dust can
Well content a craving man;
Any orts the elves refuse
Well will serve the beggar's use.
But if this may seem too much
For an alms, then give me such
Little bits that nestle there
In the pris'ner's pannier.
So a blessing light upon
You, and mighty Oberon;
That your plenty last till when
I return your alms again.

42

THE HAG

The Hag is astride,
This night for to ride,
The devil and she together;
Through thick and through thin,
Now out, and then in,
Though ne'er so foul be the weather.

A thorn or a bur
She takes for a spur;
With a lash of a bramble she rides now,
Through brakes and through briars,
O'er ditches and mires,
She follows the spirit that guides now.

No beast, for his food,
Dares now range the wood,
But hush'd in his lair he lies lurking;
While mischiefs, by these,
On land and on seas,
At noon of night are a-working.

The storm will arise,
And trouble the skies
This night; and, more for the wonder,
The ghost from the tomb
Affrighted shall come,
Call'd out by the clap of the thunder.

43

THE MAD MAID'S SONG

Good morrow to the day so fair;
Good morning, sir, to you;
Good morrow to mine own torn hair,
Bedabbled with the dew.

Good morning to this primrose too;
Good morrow to each maid;

That will with flowers the tomb bestrew
Wherein my Love is laid.

Ah! woe is me, woe, woe is me,
Alack and well-a-day!
For pity, sir, find out that bee,
Which bore my Love away.

I'll seek him in your bonnet brave;
I'll seek him in your eyes;
Nay, now I think they've made his grave
I' th' bed of strawberries.

I'll seek him there; I know, ere this,
The cold, cold earth doth shake him;
But I will go, or send a kiss
By you, sir, to awake him.

Pray hurt him not; though he be dead,
He knows well who do love him;
And who with green turfs rear his head,
And who do rudely move him.

He's soft and tender, pray take heed,
With bands of cowslips bind him,
And bring him home;--but 'tis decreed
That I shall never find him.

44

THE CHEAT OF CUPID; OR, THE UNGENTLE GUEST

One silent night of late,
When every creature rested,
Came one unto my gate,
And knocking, me molested.

Who's that, said I, beats there,
And troubles thus the sleepy?
Cast off; said he, all fear,
And let not locks thus keep ye.

For I a boy am, who
By moonless nights have swerved;
And all with showers wet through,
And e'en with cold half starved.

I pitiful arose,
And soon a taper lighted;
And did myself disclose
Unto the lad benighted.

I saw he had a bow,
And wings too, which did shiver;
And looking down below,
I spied he had a quiver.

I to my chimney's shine
Brought him, as Love professes,
And chafed his hands with mine,
And dried his dropping tresses.

But when he felt him warm'd,
Let's try this bow of ours
And string, if they be harm'd,

Said he, with these late showers.

Forthwith his bow he bent,
And wedded string and arrow,
And struck me, that it went
Quite through my heart and marrow

Then laughing loud, he flew
Away, and thus said flying,
Adieu, mine host, adieu,
I'll leave thy heart a-dying.

45

UPON CUPID

Love, like a gipsy, lately came,
And did me much importune
To see my hand, that by the same
He might foretell my fortune.

He saw my palm; and then, said he,
I tell thee, by this score here,
That thou, within few months, shalt be
The youthful Prince D'Amour here.

I smiled, and bade him once more prove,
And by some cross-line show it,
That I could ne'er be Prince of Love,
Though here the Princely Poet.

46

TO BE MERRY

Let's now take our time,
While we're in our prime,
And old, old age is afar off;
For the evil, evil days
Will come on apace,
Before we can be aware of.

47

UPON HIS GRAY HAIRS

Fly me not, though I be gray,
Lady, this I know you'll say;
Better look the roses red,
When with white commingled.
Black your hairs are; mine are white;
This begets the more delight,
When things meet most opposite;
As in pictures we descry
Venus standing Vulcan by.

48

AN HYMN TO THE MUSES

Honour to you who sit
Near to the well of wit,

And drink your fill of it!

Glory and worship be
To you, sweet Maids, thrice three,
Who still inspire me;

And teach me how to sing
Unto the lyric string,
My measures ravishing!

Then, while I sing your praise,
My priest-hood crown with bays
Green to the end of days!

49

THE COMING OF GOOD LUCK

So Good-Luck came, and on my roof did light,
Like noiseless snow, or as the dew of night;
Not all at once, but gently,--as the trees
Are by the sun-beams, tickled by degrees.

50

HIS CONTENT IN THE COUNTRY

HERE, Here I live with what my board
Can with the smallest cost afford;
Though ne'er so mean the viands be,
They well content my Prue and me:

Or pea or bean, or wort or beet,
Whatever comes, Content makes sweet.
Here we rejoice, because no rent
We pay for our poor tenement;
Wherein we rest, and never fear
The landlord or the usurer.
The quarter-day does ne'er affright
Our peaceful slumbers in the night:
We eat our own, and batten more,
Because we feed on no man's score;
But pity those whose flanks grow great,
Swell'd with the lard of other's meat.
We bless our fortunes, when we see
Our own beloved privacy;
And like our living, where we're known
To very few, or else to none.

51

HIS RETURN TO LONDON

From the dull confines of the drooping west,
To see the day spring from the pregnant east,
Ravish'd in spirit, I come, nay more, I fly
To thee, blest place of my nativity!
Thus, thus with hallow'd foot I touch the ground,
With thousand blessings by thy fortune crown'd.
O fruitful Genius! that bestowest here
An everlasting plenty year by year;
O place! O people! manners! framed to please
All nations, customs, kindreds, languages!
I am a free-born Roman; suffer then

That I amongst you live a citizen.
London my home is; though by hard fate sent
Into a long and irksome banishment;
Yet since call'd back, henceforward let me be,
O native country, repossess'd by thee!
For, rather than I'll to the west return,
I'll beg of thee first here to have mine urn.
Weak I am grown, and must in short time fall;
Give thou my sacred reliques burial.

52

HIS DESIRE

Give me a man that is not dull,
When all the world with rifts is full;
But unamazed dares clearly sing,
Whenas the roof's a-tottering;
And though it falls, continues still
Tickling the Cittern with his quill.

53

AN ODE FOR BEN JONSON

Ah Ben!
Say how or when
Shall we, thy guests,
Meet at those lyric feasts,
Made at the Sun,
The Dog, the Triple Tun;

Where we such clusters had,
As made us nobly wild, not mad?
And yet each verse of thine
Out-did the meat, out-did the frolic wine.

My Ben!
Or come again,
Or send to us
Thy wit's great overplus;
But teach us yet
Wisely to husband it,
Lest we that talent spend;
And having once brought to an end
That precious stock,--the store
Of such a wit the world should have no more.

54

TO LIVE MERRILY,
AND TO TRUST TO GOOD VERSES

Now is the time for mirth;
Nor cheek or tongue be dumb;
For with [the] flowery earth
The golden pomp is come.

The golden pomp is come;
For now each tree does wear,
Made of her pap and gum,
Rich beads of amber here.

Now reigns the Rose, and now

Th' Arabian dew besmears
My uncontrolled brow,
And my retorted hairs.

Homer, this health to thee!
In sack of such a kind,
That it would make thee see,
Though thou wert ne'er so blind

Next, Virgil I'll call forth,
To pledge this second health
In wine, whose each cup's worth
An Indian commonwealth.

A goblet next I'll drink
To Ovid; and suppose
Made he the pledge, he'd think
The world had all one nose.

Then this immensive cup
Of aromatic wine,
Catullus! I quaff up
To that terse muse of thine.

Wild I am now with heat:
O Bacchus! cool thy rays;
Or frantic I shall eat
Thy Thyrse, and bite the Bays!

Round, round, the roof does run;
And being ravish'd thus,
Come, I will drink a tun
To my Propertius.

Now, to Tibullus next,
This flood I drink to thee;
--But stay, I see a text,
That this presents to me.

Behold! Tibullus lies
Here burnt, whose small return
Of ashes scarce suffice
To fill a little urn.

Trust to good verses then;
They only will aspire,
When pyramids, as men,
Are lost i' th' funeral fire.

And when all bodies meet
In Lethe to be drown'd;
Then only numbers sweet
With endless life are crown'd.

55

THE APPARITION OF HIS, MISTRESS,
CALLING HIM TO ELYSIUM

DESUNT NONNULLA--

Come then, and like two doves with silvery wings,
Let our souls fly to th' shades, wherever springs
Sit smiling in the meads; where balm and oil,
Roses and cassia, crown the untill'd soil;

Where no disease reigns, or infection comes
To blast the air, but amber-gris and gums.
This, that, and ev'ry thicket doth transpire
More sweet than storax from the hallow'd fire;
Where ev'ry tree a wealthy issue bears
Of fragrant apples, blushing plums, or pears;
And all the shrubs, with sparkling spangles, shew
Like morning sun-shine, tinselling the dew.
Here in green meadows sits eternal May,
Purfling the margents, while perpetual day
So double-gilds the air, as that no night
Can ever rust th' enamel of the light:
Here naked younglings, handsome striplings, run
Their goals for virgins' kisses; which when done,
Then unto dancing forth the learned round
Commix'd they meet, with endless roses crown'd.
And here we'll sit on primrose-banks, and see
Love's chorus led by Cupid; and we'll he
Two loving followers too unto the grove,
Where poets sing the stories of our love.
There thou shalt hear divine Musaeus sing
Of Hero and Leander; then I'll bring
Thee to the stand, where honour'd Homer reads
His Odyssees and his high Iliads;
About whose throne the crowd of poets throng
To hear the incantation of his tongue:
To Linus, then to Pindar; and that done,
I'll bring thee, Herrick, to Anacreon,
Quaffing his full-crown'd bowls of burning wine,
And in his raptures speaking lines of thine,
Like to his subject; and as his frantic
Looks shew him truly Bacchanalian like,
Besmear'd with grapes,--welcome he shall thee thither,

Where both may rage, both drink and dance together.
Then stately Virgil, witty Ovid, by
Whom fair Corinna sits, and doth comply
With ivory wrists his laureat head, and steeps
His eye in dew of kisses while he sleeps.
Then soft Catullus, sharp-fang'd Martial,
And towering Lucan, Horace, Juvenal,
And snaky Persius; these, and those whom rage,
Dropt for the jars of heaven, fill'd, t' engage
All times unto their frenzies; thou shalt there
Behold them in a spacious theatre:
Among which glories, crown'd with sacred bays
And flatt'ring ivy, two recite their plays,
Beaumont and Fletcher, swans, to whom all ears
Listen, while they, like sirens in their spheres,
Sing their Evadne; and still more for thee
There yet remains to know than thou canst see
By glimm'ring of a fancy; Do but come,
And there I'll shew thee that capacious room
In which thy father, Jonson, now is placed
As in a globe of radiant fire, and graced
To be in that orb crown'd, that doth include
Those prophets of the former magnitude,
And he one chief. But hark! I hear the cock,
The bell-man of the night, proclaim the clock
Of late struck One; and now I see the prime
Of day break from the pregnant east:--'tis time
I vanish:--more I had to say,
But night determines here; Away!

56

THE INVITATION

To sup with thee thou didst me home invite,
And mad'st a promise that mine appetite
Should meet and tire, on such lautitious meat,
The like not Heliogabalus did eat:
And richer wine would'st give to me, thy guest,
Than Roman Sylla pour'd out at his feast.
I came, 'tis true, and look'd for fowl of price,
The bastard Phoenix; bird of Paradise;
And for no less than aromatic wine
Of maidens-blush, commix'd with jessamine.
Clean was the hearth, the mantle larded jet,
Which, wanting Lar and smoke, hung weeping wet;
At last i' th' noon of winter, did appear
A ragg'd soused neats-foot, with sick vinegar;
And in a burnish'd flagonet, stood by
Beer small as comfort, dead as charity.
At which amazed, and pond'ring on the food,
How cold it was, and how it chill'd my blood,
I curst the master, and I damn'd the souce,
And swore I'd got the ague of the house.
--Well, when to eat thou dost me next desire,
I'll bring a fever, since thou keep'st no fire.

57

TO SIR CLIPSBY CREW

Since to the country first I came,
I have lost my former flame;
And, methinks, I not inherit,

As I did, my ravish'd spirit.
If I write a verse or two,
'Tis with very much ado;
In regard I want that wine
Which should conjure up a line.
Yet, though now of Muse bereft,
I have still the manners left
For to thank you, noble sir,
For those gifts you do confer
Upon him, who only can
Be in prose a grateful man.

58

A COUNTRY LIFE:
TO HIS BROTHER, MR THOMAS HERRICK

Thrice, and above, blest, my soul's half, art thou,
In thy both last and better vow;
Could'st leave the city, for exchange, to see
The country's sweet simplicity;
And it to know and practise, with intent
To grow the sooner innocent;
By studying to know virtue, and to aim
More at her nature than her name;
The last is but the least; the first doth tell
Ways less to live, than to live well:--
And both are known to thee, who now canst live
Led by thy conscience, to give
Justice to soon-pleased nature, and to show
Wisdom and she together go,
And keep one centre; This with that conspires

To teach man to confine desires,
And know that riches have their proper stint
In the contented mind, not mint;
And canst instruct that those who have the itch
Of craving more, are never rich.
These things thou knows't to th' height, and dost prevent
That plague, because thou art content
With that Heaven gave thee with a wary hand,
(More blessed in thy brass than land)
To keep cheap Nature even and upright;
To cool, not cocker appetite.
Thus thou canst tersely live to satisfy
The belly chiefly, not the eye;
Keeping the barking stomach wisely quiet,
Less with a neat than needful diet.
But that which most makes sweet thy country life,
Is the fruition of a wife,
Whom, stars consenting with thy fate, thou hast
Got not so beautiful as chaste;
By whose warm side thou dost securely sleep,
While Love the sentinel doth keep,
With those deeds done by day, which ne'er affright
Thy silken slumbers in the night:
Nor has the darkness power to usher in
Fear to those sheets that know no sin.
The damask'd meadows and the pebbly streams
Sweeten and make soft your dreams:
The purling springs, groves, birds, and well weaved bowers,
With fields enamelled with flowers,
Present their shapes, while fantasy discloses
Millions of Lilies mix'd with Roses.
Then dream, ye hear the lamb by many a bleat
Woo'd to come suck the milky teat;

While Faunus in the vision comes, to keep
From rav'ning wolves the fleecy sheep:
With thousand such enchanting dreams, that meet
To make sleep not so sound as sweet;
Nor call these figures so thy rest endear,
As not to rise when Chanticlere
Warns the last watch;--but with the dawn dost rise
To work, but first to sacrifice;
Making thy peace with Heaven for some late fault,
With holy-meal and spirting salt;
Which done, thy painful thumb this sentence tells us,
'Jove for our labour all things sells us.'
Nor are thy daily and devout affairs
Attended with those desp'rate cares
Th' industrious merchant has, who for to find
Gold, runneth to the Western Ind,
And back again, tortured with fears, doth fly,
Untaught to suffer Poverty;--
But thou at home, blest with securest ease,
Sitt'st, and believ'st that there be seas,
And watery dangers; while thy whiter hap
But sees these things within thy map;
And viewing them with a more safe survey,
Mak'st easy fear unto thee say,
'A heart thrice walled with oak and brass, that man
Had, first durst plough the ocean.'
But thou at home, without or tide or gale,
Canst in thy map securely sail;
Seeing those painted countries, and so guess
By those fine shades, their substances;
And from thy compass taking small advice,
Buy'st travel at the lowest price.
Nor are thine ears so deaf but thou canst hear,

Far more with wonder than with fear,
Fame tell of states, of countries, courts, and kings,
And believe there be such things;
When of these truths thy happier knowledge lies
More in thine ears than in thine eyes.
And when thou hear'st by that too true report,
Vice rules the most, or all, at court,
Thy pious wishes are, though thou not there,
Virtue had, and moved her sphere.
But thou liv'st fearless; and thy face ne'er shows
Fortune when she comes, or goes;
But with thy equal thoughts, prepared dost stand
To take her by the either hand;
Nor car'st which comes the first, the foul or fair:--
A wise man ev'ry way lies square;
And like a surly oak with storms perplex'd
Grows still the stronger, strongly vex'd.
Be so, bold Spirit; stand centre-like, unmoved;
And be not only thought, but proved
To be what I report thee, and inure
Thyself, if want comes, to endure;
And so thou dost; for thy desires are
Confined to live with private Lar:
Nor curious whether appetite be fed
Or with the first, or second bread.
Who keep'st no proud mouth for delicious cates;
Hunger makes coarse meats, delicates.
Canst, and unurged, forsake that larded fare,
Which art, not nature, makes so rare;
To taste boil'd nettles, coleworts, beets, and eat
These, and sour herbs, as dainty meat:--
While soft opinion makes thy Genius say,
'Content makes all ambrosia;'

Nor is it that thou keep'st this stricter size
So much for want, as exercise;
To numb the sense of dearth, which, should sin haste it,
Thou might'st but only see't, not taste it;
Yet can thy humble roof maintain a quire
Of singing crickets by thy fire;
And the brisk mouse may feast herself with crumbs,
Till that the green-eyed kitling comes;
Then to her cabin, blest she can escape
The sudden danger of a rape.
--And thus thy little well-kept stock doth prove,
Wealth cannot make a life, but love.
Nor art thou so close-handed, but canst spend,
(Counsel concurring with the end),
As well as spare; still conning o'er this theme,
To shun the first and last extreme;
Ordaining that thy small stock find no breach,
Or to exceed thy tether's reach;
But to live round, and close, and wisely true
To thine own self, and known to few.
Thus let thy rural sanctuary be
Elysium to thy wife and thee;
There to disport your selves with golden measure;
For seldom use commends the pleasure.
Live, and live blest; thrice happy pair; let breath,
But lost to one, be th' other's death:
And as there is one love, one faith, one troth,
Be so one death, one grave to both;
Till when, in such assurance live, ye may
Nor fear, or wish your dying day.

TO HIS PECULIAR FRIEND, MR JOHN WICKS

Since shed or cottage I have none,
I sing the more, that thou hast one;
To whose glad threshold, and free door
I may a Poet come, though poor;
And eat with thee a savoury bit,
Paying but common thanks for it.
--Yet should I chance, my Wicks, to see
An over-leaven look in thee,
To sour the bread, and turn the beer
To an exalted vinegar;
Or should'st thou prize me as a dish
Of thrice-boil'd worts, or third-day's fish,
I'd rather hungry go and come
Than to thy house be burdensome;
Yet, in my depth of grief, I'd be
One that should drop his beads for thee.

60

A PARANAETICALL, OR ADVISIVE VERSE
TO HIS FRIEND, MR JOHN WICKS

Is this a life, to break thy sleep,
To rise as soon as day doth peep?
To tire thy patient ox or ass
By noon, and let thy good days pass,
Not knowing this, that Jove decrees
Some mirth, t' adulce man's miseries?
--No; 'tis a life to have thine oil

Without extortion from thy soil;
Thy faithful fields to yield thee grain,
Although with some, yet little pain;
To have thy mind, and nuptial bed,
With fears and cares uncumbered
A pleasing wife, that by thy side
Lies softly panting like a bride;
--This is to live, and to endear
Those minutes Time has lent us here.
Then, while fates suffer, live thou free,
As is that air that circles thee;
And crown thy temples too; and let
Thy servant, not thy own self, sweat,
To strut thy barns with sheaves of wheat.
--Time steals away like to a stream,
And we glide hence away with them:
No sound recalls the hours once fled,
Or roses, being withered;
Nor us, my friend, when we are lost,
Like to a dew, or melted frost.
--Then live we mirthful while we should,
And turn the iron age to gold;
Let's feast and frolic, sing and play,
And thus less last, than live our day.
Whose life with care is overcast,
That man's not said to live, but last;
Nor is't a life, seven years to tell,
But for to live that half seven well;
And that we'll do, as men who know,
Some few sands spent, we hence must go,
Both to be blended in the urn,
From whence there's never a return.

61

TO HIS HONOURED AND MOST INGENIOUS FRIEND
MR CHARLES COTTON

For brave comportment, wit without offence,
Words fully flowing, yet of influence,
Thou art that man of men, the man alone
Worthy the public admiration;
Who with thine own eyes read'st what we do write,
And giv'st our numbers euphony and weight;
Tell'st when a verse springs high; how understood
To be, or not, born of the royal blood
What state above, what symmetry below,
Lines have, or should have, thou the best can show:--
For which, my Charles, it is my pride to be,
Not so much known, as to be loved of thee:--
Long may I live so, and my wreath of bays
Be less another's laurel, than thy praise.

62

A NEW YEAR'S GIFT,
SENT TO SIR SIMEON STEWARD

No news of navies burnt at seas;
No noise of late spawn'd tittyries;
No closet plot or open vent,
That frights men with a Parliament:
No new device or late-found trick,
To read by th' stars the kingdom's sick;

No gin to catch the State, or wring
The free-born nostril of the King,
We send to you; but here a jolly
Verse crown'd with ivy and with holly;
That tells of winter's tales and mirth
That milk-maids make about the hearth;
Of Christmas sports, the wassail-bowl,
That toss'd up, after Fox-i'-th'-hole;
Of Blind-man-buff, and of the care
That young men have to shoe the Mare;
Of twelf-tide cakes, of pease and beans,
Wherewith ye make those merry scenes,
Whenas ye chuse your king and queen,
And cry out, 'Hey for our town green!'--
Of ash-heaps, in the which ye use
Husbands and wives by streaks to chuse;
Of crackling laurel, which fore-sounds
A plenteous harvest to your grounds;
Of these, and such like things, for shift,
We send instead of New-year's gift.
--Read then, and when your faces shine
With buxom meat and cap'ring wine,
Remember us in cups full crown'd,
And let our city-health go round,
Quite through the young maids and the men,
To the ninth number, if not ten;
Until the fired chestnuts leap
For joy to see the fruits ye reap,
From the plump chalice and the cup
That tempts till it be tossed up.--
Then as ye sit about your embers,
Call not to mind those fled Decembers;
But think on these, that are t' appear,

As daughters to the instant year;
Sit crown'd with rose-buds, and carouse,
Till LIBER PATER twirls the house
About your ears, and lay upon
The year, your cares, that's fled and gone:
And let the russet swains the plough
And harrow hang up resting now;
And to the bag-pipe all address,
Till sleep takes place of weariness.
And thus throughout, with Christmas plays,
Frolic the full twelve holy-days.

63

AN ODE TO SIR CLIPSBY CREW

Here we securely live, and eat
The cream of meat;
And keep eternal fires,
By which we sit, and do divine,
As wine
And rage inspires.

If full, we charm; then call upon
Anacreon
To grace the frantic Thyrse:
And having drunk, we raise a shout
Throughout,
To praise his verse.

Then cause we Horace to be read,
Which sung or said,

A goblet, to the brim,
Of lyric wine, both swell'd and crown'd,
Around
We quaff to him.

Thus, thus we live, and spend the hours
In wine and flowers;
And make the frolic year,
The month, the week, the instant day
To stay
The longer here.

--Come then, brave Knight, and see the cell
Wherein I dwell;
And my enchantments too;
Which love and noble freedom is:--
And this
Shall fetter you.

Take horse, and come; or be so kind
To send your mind,
Though but in numbers few:--
And I shall think I have the heart
Or part
Of Clipsby Crew.

64

A PANEGYRIC TO SIR LEWIS PEMBERTON

Till I shall come again, let this suffice,
I send my salt, my sacrifice

To thee, thy lady, younglings, and as far
As to thy Genius and thy Lar;
To the worn threshold, porch, hall, parlour, kitchen,
The fat-fed smoking temple, which in
The wholesome savour of thy mighty chines,
Invites to supper him who dines:
Where laden spits, warp'd with large ribs of beef,
Not represent, but give relief
To the lank stranger and the sour swain,
Where both may feed and come again;
For no black-bearded Vigil from thy door
Beats with a button'd-staff the poor;
But from thy warm love-hatching gates, each may
Take friendly morsels, and there stay
To sun his thin-clad members, if he likes;
For thou no porter keep'st who strikes.
No comer to thy roof his guest-rite wants;
Or, staying there, is scourged with taunts
Of some rough groom, who, yirk'd with corns, says, 'Sir,
'You've dipp'd too long i' th' vinegar;
'And with our broth and bread and bits, Sir friend,
'You've fared well; pray make an end;
'Two days you've larded here; a third, ye know,
'Makes guests and fish smell strong; pray go
'You to some other chimney, and there take
'Essay of other giblets; make
'Merry at another's hearth; you're here
'Welcome as thunder to our beer;
'Manners knows distance, and a man unrude
'Would soon recoil, and not intrude
'His stomach to a second meal.'--No, no,
Thy house, well fed and taught, can show
No such crabb'd vizard: Thou hast learnt thy train

With heart and hand to entertain;
And by the arms-full, with a breast unhid,
As the old race of mankind did,
When either's heart, and either's hand did strive
To be the nearer relative;
Thou dost redeem those times: and what was lost
Of ancient honesty, may boast
It keeps a growth in thee, and so will run
A course in thy fame's pledge, thy son.
Thus, like a Roman Tribune, thou thy gate
Early sets ope to feast, and late;
Keeping no currish waiter to affright,
With blasting eye, the appetite,
Which fain would waste upon thy cates, but that
The trencher creature marketh what
Best and more suppling piece he cuts, and by
Some private pinch tells dangers nigh,
A hand too desp'rate, or a knife that bites
Skin-deep into the pork, or lights
Upon some part of kid, as if mistook,
When checked by the butler's look.
No, no, thy bread, thy wine, thy jocund beer
Is not reserved for Trebius here,
But all who at thy table seated are,
Find equal freedom, equal fare;
And thou, like to that hospitable god,
Jove, joy'st when guests make their abode
To eat thy bullocks thighs, thy veals, thy fat
Wethers, and never grudged at.
The pheasant, partridge, gotwit, reeve, ruff, rail,
The cock, the curlew, and the quail,
These, and thy choicest viands, do extend
Their tastes unto the lower end

Of thy glad table; not a dish more known
To thee, than unto any one:
But as thy meat, so thy immortal wine
Makes the smirk face of each to shine,
And spring fresh rose-buds, while the salt, the wit,
Flows from the wine, and graces it;
While Reverence, waiting at the bashful board,
Honours my lady and my lord.
No scurril jest, no open scene is laid
Here, for to make the face afraid;
But temp'rate mirth dealt forth, and so discreet-
Ly, that it makes the meat more sweet,
And adds perfumes unto the wine, which thou
Dost rather pour forth, than allow
By cruse and measure; thus devoting wine,
As the Canary isles were thine;
But with that wisdom and that method, as
No one that's there his guilty glass
Drinks of distemper, or has cause to cry
Repentance to his liberty.
No, thou know'st orders, ethics, and hast read
All oeconomics, know'st to lead
A house-dance neatly, and canst truly show
How far a figure ought to go,
Forward or backward, side-ward, and what pace
Can give, and what retract a grace;
What gesture, courtship, comeliness agrees,
With those thy primitive decrees,
To give subsistence to thy house, and proof
What Genii support thy roof,
Goodness and greatness, not the oaken piles;
For these, and marbles have their whiles
To last, but not their ever; virtue's hand

It is which builds 'gainst fate to stand.
Such is thy house, whose firm foundations trust
Is more in thee than in her dust,
Or depth; these last may yield, and yearly shrink,
When what is strongly built, no chink
Or yawning rupture can the same devour,
But fix'd it stands, by her own power
And well-laid bottom, on the iron and rock,
Which tries, and counter-stands the shock
And ram of time, and by vexation grows
The stronger. Virtue dies when foes
Are wanting to her exercise, but, great
And large she spreads by dust and sweat.
Safe stand thy walls, and thee, and so both will,
Since neither's height was raised by th'ill
Of others; since no stud, no stone, no piece
Was rear'd up by the poor-man's fleece;
No widow's tenement was rack'd to gild
Or fret thy cieling, or to build
A sweating-closet, to anoint the silk-
Soft skin, or bath[e] in asses' milk;
No orphan's pittance, left him, served to set
The pillars up of lasting jet,
For which their cries might beat against thine ears,
Or in the damp jet read their tears.
No plank from hallow'd altar does appeal
To yond' Star-chamber, or does seal
A curse to thee, or thine; but all things even
Make for thy peace, and pace to heaven.
--Go on directly so, as just men may
A thousand times more swear, than say
This is that princely Pemberton, who can
Teach men to keep a God in man;

And when wise poets shall search out to see
Good men, they find them all in thee.

65

ALL THINGS DECAY AND DIE

All things decay with time: The forest sees
The growth and down-fall of her aged trees;
That timber tall, which three-score lustres stood
The proud dictator of the state-like wood,
I mean the sovereign of all plants, the oak,
Droops, dies, and falls without the cleaver's stroke.

66

TO HIS DYING BROTHER, MASTER WILLIAM HERRICK

Life of my life, take not so soon thy flight,
But stay the time till we have bade good-night.
Thou hast both wind and tide with thee; thy way
As soon dispatch'd is by the night as day.
Let us not then so rudely henceforth go
Till we have wept, kiss'd, sigh'd, shook hands, or so.
There's pain in parting, and a kind of hell
When once true lovers take their last farewell.
What? shall we two our endless leaves take here
Without a sad look, or a solemn tear?
He knows not love that hath not this truth proved,
Love is most loth to leave the thing beloved.
Pay we our vows and go; yet when we part,

Then, even then, I will bequeath my heart
Into thy loving hands; for I'll keep none
To warm my breast, when thou, my pulse, art gone,
No, here I'll last, and walk, a harmless shade,
About this urn, wherein thy dust is laid,
To guard it so, as nothing here shall be
Heavy, to hurt those sacred seeds of thee.

67

HIS AGE:
DEDICATED TO HIS PECULIAR FRIEND,
MR JOHN WICKES, UNDER THE NAME OF
POSTUMUS

Ah, Posthumus! our years hence fly
And leave no sound: nor piety,
Or prayers, or vow
Can keep the wrinkle from the brow;
But we must on,
As fate does lead or draw us; none,
None, Posthumus, could e'er decline
The doom of cruel Proserpine.

The pleasing wife, the house, the ground
Must all be left, no one plant found
To follow thee,
Save only the curst cypress-tree!
--A merry mind
Looks forward, scorns what's left behind;
Let's live, my Wickes, then, while we may,
And here enjoy our holiday.

We've seen the past best times, and these
Will ne'er return; we see the seas,
And moons to wane,
But they fill up their ebbs again;
But vanish'd man,
Like to a lily lost, ne'er can,
Ne'er can repullulate, or bring
His days to see a second spring.

But on we must, and thither tend,
Where Ancus and rich Tullus blend
Their sacred seed;
Thus has infernal Jove decreed;
We must be made,
Ere long a song, ere long a shade.
Why then, since life to us is short,
Let's make it full up by our sport.

Crown we our heads with roses then,
And 'noint with Tyrian balm; for when
We two are dead,
The world with us is buried.
Then live we free
As is the air, and let us be
Our own fair wind, and mark each one
Day with the white and lucky stone.

We are not poor, although we have
No roofs of cedar, nor our brave
Baiae, nor keep
Account of such a flock of sheep;
Nor bullocks fed

To lard the shambles; barbels bred
To kiss our hands; nor do we wish
For Pollio's lampreys in our dish.

If we can meet, and so confer,
Both by a shining salt-cellar,
And have our roof,
Although not arch'd, yet weather-proof,
And cieling free,
From that cheap candle-baudery;
We'll eat our bean with that full mirth
As we were lords of all the earth.

Well, then, on what seas we are tost,
Our comfort is, we can't be lost.
Let the winds drive
Our bark, yet she will keep alive
Amidst the deeps;
'Tis constancy, my Wickes, which keeps
The pinnace up; which, though she errs
I' th' seas, she saves her passengers.

Say, we must part; sweet mercy bless
Us both i' th' sea, camp, wilderness!
Can we so far
Stray, to become less circular
Than we are now?
No, no, that self-same heart, that vow
Which made us one, shall ne'er undo,
Or ravel so, to make us two.

Live in thy peace; as for myself,
When I am bruised on the shelf

Of time, and show
My locks behung with frost and snow;
When with the rheum,
The cough, the pthisic, I consume
Unto an almost nothing; then,
The ages fled, I'll call again,

And with a tear compare these last
Lame and bad times with those are past,
While Baucis by,
My old lean wife, shall kiss it dry;
And so we'll sit
By th' fire, foretelling snow and slit
And weather by our aches, grown
Now old enough to be our own

True calendars, as puss's ear
Wash'd o'er 's, to tell what change is near;
Then to assuage
The gripings of the chine by age,
I'll call my young
Iulus to sing such a song
I made upon my Julia's breast,
And of her blush at such a feast.

Then shall he read that flower of mine
Enclosed within a crystal shrine;
A primrose next;
A piece then of a higher text;
For to beget
In me a more transcendant heat,
Than that insinuating fire
Which crept into each aged sire

When the fair Helen from her eyes
Shot forth her loving sorceries;
At which I'll rear
Mine aged limbs above my chair;
And hearing it,
Flutter and crow, as in a fit
Of fresh concupiscence, and cry,
'No lust there's like to Poetry.'

Thus frantic, crazy man, God wot,
I'll call to mind things half-forgot;
And oft between
Repeat the times that I have seen;
Thus ripe with tears,
And twisting my Iulus' hairs,
Doting, I'll weep and say, 'In truth,
Baucis, these were my sins of youth.'

Then next I'll cause my hopeful lad,
If a wild apple can be had,
To crown the hearth;
Lar thus conspiring with our mirth;
Then to infuse
Our browner ale into the cruse;
Which, sweetly spiced, we'll first carouse
Unto the Genius of the house.

Then the next health to friends of mine.
Loving the brave Burgundian wine,
High sons of pith,
Whose fortunes I have frolick'd with;
Such as could well

Bear up the magic bough and spell;
And dancing 'bout the mystic Thyrse,
Give up the just applause to verse;

To those, and then again to thee,
We'll drink, my Wickes, until we be
Plump as the cherry,
Though not so fresh, yet full as merry
As the cricket,
The untamed heifer, or the pricket,
Until our tongues shall tell our ears,
We're younger by a score of years.

Thus, till we see the fire less shine
From th' embers than the kitling's eyne,
We'll still sit up,
Sphering about the wassail cup,
To all those times
Which gave me honour for my rhymes;
The coal once spent, we'll then to bed,
Far more than night bewearied.

68

THE BAD SEASON MAKES THE POET SAD

Dull to myself, and almost dead to these,
My many fresh and fragrant mistresses;
Lost to all music now, since every thing
Puts on the semblance here of sorrowing.
Sick is the land to th' heart; and doth endure
More dangerous faintings by her desperate cure.

But if that golden age would come again,
And Charles here rule, as he before did reign;
If smooth and unperplex'd the seasons were,
As when the sweet Maria lived here;
I should delight to have my curls half drown'd
In Tyrian dews, and head with roses crown'd:
And once more yet, ere I am laid out dead,
Knock at a star with my exalted head.

69

ON HIMSELF

A wearied pilgrim I have wander'd here,
Twice five-and-twenty, bate me but one year;
Long I have lasted in this world; 'tis true
But yet those years that I have lived, but few.
Who by his gray hairs doth his lustres tell,
Lives not those years, but he that lives them well:
One man has reach'd his sixty years, but he
Of all those three-score has not lived half three:
He lives who lives to virtue; men who cast
Their ends for pleasure, do not live, but last.

70

HIS WINDING-SHEET

Come thou, who art the wine and wit
Of all I've writ;
The grace, the glory, and the best

Piece of the rest;
Thou art of what I did intend
The All, and End;
And what was made, was made to meet.
Thee, thee my sheet.
Come then, and be to my chaste side
Both bed and bride.
We two, as reliques left, will have
One rest, one grave;
And, hugging close, we need not fear
Lust entering here,
Where all desires are dead or cold,
As is the mould;
And all affections are forgot,
Or trouble not.
Here, here the slaves and prisoners be
From shackles free;
And weeping widows, long opprest,
Do here find rest.
The wronged client ends his laws
Here, and his cause;
Here those long suits of Chancery lie
Quiet, or die;
And all Star-chamber bills do cease,
Or hold their peace.
Here needs no court for our Request
Where all are best;
All wise, all equal, and all just
Alike i'th' dust.
Nor need we here to fear the frown
Of court or crown;
Where fortune bears no sway o'er things,
There all are kings.

In this securer place we'll keep,
As lull'd asleep;
Or for a little time we'll lie,
As robes laid by,
To be another day re-worn,
Turn'd, but not torn;
Or like old testaments engrost,
Lock'd up, not lost;
And for a-while lie here conceal'd,
To be reveal'd
Next, at that great Platonic year,
And then meet here.

71

ANACREONTIC

Born I was to be old,
And for to die here;
After that, in the mould
Long for to lie here.
But before that day comes,
Still I be bousing;
For I know, in the tombs
There's no carousing.

72

TO LAURELS

A funeral stone

Or verse, I covet none;
But only crave
Of you that I may have
A sacred laurel springing from my grave:
Which being seen
Blest with perpetual green,
May grow to be
Not so much call'd a tree,
As the eternal monument of me.

73

ON HIMSELF

Weep for the dead, for they have lost this light;
And weep for me, lost in an endless night;
Or mourn, or make a marble verse for me,
Who writ for many. BENEDICTE.

74

ON HIMSELF

Lost to the world; lost to myself; alone
Here now I rest under this marble stone,
In depth of silence, heard and seen of none.

75

TO ROBIN RED-BREAST

Laid out for dead, let thy last kindness be
With leaves and moss-work for to cover me;
And while the wood-nymphs my cold corpse inter,
Sing thou my dirge, sweet-warbling chorister!
For epitaph, in foliage, next write this:
HERE, HERE THE TOMB OF ROBIN HERRICK IS!

76

THE OLIVE BRANCH

Sadly I walk'd within the field,
To see what comfort it would yield;
And as I went my private way,
An olive-branch before me lay;
And seeing it, I made a stay,
And took it up, and view'd it; then
Kissing the omen, said Amen;
Be, be it so, and let this be
A divination unto me;
That in short time my woes shall cease,
And love shall crown my end with peace.

77

THE PLAUDITE, OR END OF LIFE

If after rude and boisterous seas
My wearied pinnace here finds ease;
If so it be I've gain'd the shore,

With safety of a faithful oar;
If having run my barque on ground,
Ye see the aged vessel crown'd;
What's to be done? but on the sands
Ye dance and sing, and now clap hands.
--The first act's doubtful, but (we say)
It is the last commends the Play.

*

AMORES

78

TO GROVES

Ye silent shades, whose each tree here
Some relique of a saint doth wear;
Who for some sweet-heart's sake, did prove
The fire and martyrdom of Love:--
Here is the legend of those saints
That died for love, and their complaints;
Their wounded hearts, and names we find
Encarved upon the leaves and rind.
Give way, give way to me, who come
Scorch'd with the self-same martyrdom!
And have deserved as much, Love knows,
As to be canonized 'mongst those
Whose deeds and deaths here written are
Within your Greeny-kalendar.
--By all those virgins' fillets hung
Upon! your boughs, and requiems sung

For saints and souls departed hence,
Here honour'd still with frankincense;
By all those tears that have been shed,
As a drink-offering to the dead;
By all those true-love knots, that be
With mottoes carved on every tree;
By sweet Saint Phillis! pity me;
By dear Saint Iphis! and the rest
Of all those other saints now blest,
Me, me forsaken,--here admit
Among your myrtles to be writ;
That my poor name may have the glory
To live remember'd in your story.

** AMORES **

79

MRS ELIZ: WHEELER, UNDER THE NAME OF THE LOST SHEPHERDESS

Among the myrtles as I walk'd
Love and my sighs thus intertalk'd:
Tell me, said I, in deep distress,
Where I may find my Shepherdess?
--Thou fool, said Love, know'st thou not this?
In every thing that's sweet she is.
In yond' carnation go and seek,
There thou shalt find her lip and cheek;
In that enamell'd pansy by,
There thou shalt have her curious eye;

In bloom of peach and rose's bud,
There waves the streamer of her blood.
--'Tis true, said I; and thereupon
I went to pluck them one by one,
To make of parts an union;
But on a sudden all were gone.
At which I stopp'd; Said Love, these be
The true resemblances of thee;
For as these flowers, thy joys must die;
And in the turning of an eye;
And all thy hopes of her must wither,
Like those short sweets here knit together.

80

A VOW TO VENUS

Happily I had a sight
Of my dearest dear last night;
Make her this day smile on me,
And I'll roses give to thee!

81

UPON LOVE

A crystal vial Cupid brought,
Which had a juice in it:
Of which who drank, he said, no thought
Of Love he should admit.

I, greedy of the prize, did drink,
And emptied soon the glass;
Which burnt me so, that I do think
The fire of hell it was.

Give me my earthen cups again,
The crystal I contemn,
Which, though enchased with pearls, contain
A deadly draught in them.

And thou, O Cupid! come not to
My threshold,--since I see,
For all I have, or else can do,
Thou still wilt cozen me.

82

UPON JULIA'S CLOTHES

Whenas in silks my Julia goes,
Till, then, methinks, how sweetly flows
That liquefaction of her clothes!
Next, when I cast mine eyes, and see
That brave vibration each way free;
O how that glittering taketh me!

83

THE BRACELET TO JULIA

Why I tie about thy wrist,

Julia, this my silken twist?
For what other reason is't,
But to shew thee how in part
Thou my pretty captive art?
But thy bond-slave is my heart;
'Tis but silk that bindeth thee,
Knap the thread and thou art free;
But 'tis otherwise with me;
I am bound, and fast bound so,
That from thee I cannot go;
If I could, I would not so.

84

UPON JULIA'S RIBBON

As shews the air when with a rain-bow graced,
So smiles that ribbon 'bout my Julia's waist;
Or like----Nay, 'tis that Zonulet of love,
Wherein all pleasures of the world are wove.

85

TO JULIA

How rich and pleasing thou, my Julia, art,
In each thy dainty and peculiar part!
First, for thy Queen-ship on thy head is set
Of flowers a sweet commingled coronet;
About thy neck a carkanet is bound,
Made of the Ruby, Pearl, and Diamond;

A golden ring, that shines upon thy thumb;
About thy wrist the rich Dardanium;
Between thy breasts, than down of swans more white,
There plays the Sapphire with the Chrysolite.
No part besides must of thyself be known,
But by the Topaz, Opal, Calcedon.

86

ART ABOVE NATURE: TO JULIA

When I behold a forest spread
With silken trees upon thy head;
And when I see that other dress
Of flowers set in comeliness;
When I behold another grace
In the ascent of curious lace,
Which, like a pinnacle, doth shew
The top, and the top-gallant too;
Then, when I see thy tresses bound
Into an oval, square, or round,
And knit in knots far more than I.
Can tell by tongue, or True-love tie;
Next, when those lawny films I see
Play with a wild civility;
And all those airy silks to flow,
Alluring me, and tempting so--
I must confess, mine eye and heart
Dotes less on nature than on art.

87

HER BED

See'st thou that cloud as silver clear,
Plump, soft, and swelling every where?
'Tis Julia's bed, and she sleeps there.

88

THE ROCK OF RUBIES, AND THE QUARRY OF PEARLS

Some ask'd me where the Rubies grew:
And nothing I did say,
But with my finger pointed to
The lips of Julia.
Some ask'd how Pearls did grow, and where:
Then spoke I to my girl,
To part her lips, and shew me there
The quarrelets of Pearl.

89

THE PARLIAMENT OF ROSES TO JULIA

I dreamt the Roses one time went
To meet and sit in Parliament;
The place for these, and for the rest
Of flowers, was thy spotless breast.
Over the which a state was drawn
Of tiffany, or cob-web lawn;

Then in that Parly all those powers
Voted the Rose the Queen of flowers;
But so, as that herself should be
The Maid of Honour unto thee.

90

UPON JULIA'S RECOVERY

Droop, droop no more, or hang the head,
Ye roses almost withered;
Now strength, and newer purple get,
Each here declining violet.
O primroses! let this day be
A resurrection unto ye;
And to all flowers allied in blood,
Or sworn to that sweet sisterhood.
For health on Julia's cheek hath shed
Claret and cream commingled;
And those, her lips, do now appear
As beams of coral, but more clear.

91

UPON JULIA'S HAIR FILLED WITH DEW

Dew sate on Julia's hair,
And spangled too,
Like leaves that laden are
With trembling dew;
Or glitter'd to my sight,

As when the beams
Have their reflected light
Danced by the streams.

92

CHERRY RIPE

Cherry-ripe, ripe, ripe, I cry,
Full and fair ones; come, and buy:
If so be you ask me where
They do grow? I answer, there
Where my Julia's lips do smile;--
There's the land, or cherry-isle;
Whose plantations fully show
All the year where cherries grow.

93

THE CAPTIVE BEE; OR, THE LITTLE FILCHER

As Julia once a-slumb'ring lay,
It chanced a bee did fly that way,
After a dew, or dew-like shower,
To tipple freely in a flower;
For some rich flower, he took the lip
Of Julia, and began to sip;
But when he felt he suck'd from thence
Honey, and in the quintessence,
He drank so much he scarce could stir;
So Julia took the pilferer.

And thus surprised, as filchers use,
He thus began himself t'excuse:
'Sweet lady-flower, I never brought
Hither the least one thieving thought;
But taking those rare lips of yours
For some fresh, fragrant, luscious flowers,
I thought I might there take a taste,
Where so much sirup ran at waste.
Besides, know this, I never sting
The flower that gives me nourishing;
But with a kiss, or thanks, do pay
For honey that I bear away.'
--This said, he laid his little scrip
Of honey 'fore her ladyship,
And told her, as some tears did fall,
That, that he took, and that was all.
At which she smiled, and bade him go
And take his bag; but thus much know,
When next he came a-pilfering so,
He should from her full lips derive
Honey enough to fill his hive.

94

UPON ROSES

Under a lawn, than skies more clear,
Some ruffled Roses nestling were,
And snugging there, they seem'd to lie
As in a flowery nunnery;
They blush'd, and look'd more fresh than flowers
Quickened of late by pearly showers;

And all, because they were possest
But of the heat of Julia's breast,
Which, as a warm and moisten'd spring,
Gave them their ever-flourishing.

95

HOW HIS SOUL CAME ENSNARED

My soul would one day go and seek
For roses, and in Julia's cheek
A richess of those sweets she found,
As in another Rosamond;
But gathering roses as she was,
Not knowing what would come to pass,
it chanced a ringlet of her hair
Caught my poor soul, as in a snare;
Which ever since has been in thrall;
--Yet freedom she enjoys withal.

96

UPON JULIA'S VOICE

When I thy singing next shall hear,
I'll wish I might turn all to ear,
To drink-in notes and numbers, such
As blessed souls can't hear too much
Then melted down, there let me lie
Entranced, and lost confusedly;
And by thy music strucken mute,

Die, and be turn'd into a Lute.

97

THE NIGHT PIECE: TO JULIA

Her eyes the glow-worm lend thee,
The shooting stars attend thee;
And the elves also,
Whose little eyes glow
Like the sparks of fire, befriend thee.

No Will-o'th'-Wisp mis-light thee,
Nor snake or slow-worm bite thee;
But on, on thy way,
Not making a stay,
Since ghost there's none to affright thee.

Let not the dark thee cumber;
What though the moon does slumber?
The stars of the night
Will lend thee their light,
Like tapers clear, without number.

Then, Julia, let me woo thee,
Thus, thus to come unto me;
And when I shall meet
Thy silvery feet,
My soul I'll pour into thee.

98

HIS COVENANT OR PROTESTATION TO JULIA

Why dost thou wound and break my heart,
As if we should for ever part?
Hast thou not heard an oath from me,
After a day, or two, or three,
I would come back and live with thee?
Take, if thou dost distrust that vow,
This second protestation now:--
Upon thy cheek that spangled tear,
Which sits as dew of roses there,
That tear shall scarce be dried before
I'll kiss the threshold of thy door;
Then weep not, Sweet, but thus much know,--
I'm half returned before I go.

99

HIS SAILING FROM JULIA

When that day comes, whose evening says I'm gone
Unto that watery desolation;
Devoutly to thy Closet-gods then pray,
That my wing'd ship may meet no Remora.
Those deities which circum-walk the seas,
And look upon our dreadful passages,
Will from all dangers re-deliver me,
For one drink-offering poured out by thee,
Mercy and Truth live with thee! and forbear,
In my short absence, to unsluice a tear;
But yet for love's-sake, let thy lips do this,--

Give my dead picture one engendering kiss;
Work that to life, and let me ever dwell
In thy remembrance, Julia. So farewell.

100

HIS LAST REQUEST TO JULIA

I have been wanton, and too bold, I fear,
To chafe o'er-much the virgin's cheek or ear;--
Beg for my pardon, Julia! he doth win
Grace with the gods who's sorry for his sin.
That done, my Julia, dearest Julia, come,
And go with me to chuse my burial room:
My fates are ended; when thy Herrick dies,
Clasp thou his book, then close thou up his eyes.

101

THE TRANSFIGURATION

Immortal clothing I put on
So soon as, Julia, I am gone
To mine eternal mansion.

Thou, thou art here, to human sight
Clothed all with incorrupted light;
--But yet how more admir'dly bright

Wilt thou appear, when thou art set
In thy refulgent thronelet,

That shin'st thus in thy counterfeit!

102

LOVE DISLIKES NOTHING

Whatsoever thing I see,
Rich or poor although it be,
--'Tis a mistress unto me.

Be my girl or fair or brown,
Does she smile, or does she frown;
Still I write a sweet-heart down.

Be she rough, or smooth of skin;
When I touch, I then begin
For to let affection in.

Be she bald, or does she wear
Locks incurl'd of other hair;
I shall find enchantment there.

Be she whole, or be she rent,
So my fancy be content,
She's to me most excellent.

Be she fat, or be she lean;
Be she sluttish, be she clean;
I'm a man for every scene.

103

UPON LOVE

I held Love's head while it did ache;
But so it chanced to be,
The cruel pain did his forsake,
And forthwith came to me.

Ai me! how shall my grief be still'd?
Or where else shall we find
One like to me, who must be kill'd
For being too-too-kind?

104

TO DIANEME

I could but see thee yesterday
Stung by a fretful bee;
And I the javelin suck'd away,
And heal'd the wound in thee.

A thousand thorns, and briars, and stings
I have in my poor breast;
Yet ne'er can see that salve which brings
My passions any rest.

As Love shall help me, I admire
How thou canst sit and smile
To see me bleed, and not desire
To staunch the blood the while.

If thou, composed of gentle mould,
Art so unkind to me;
What dismal stories will be told
Of those that cruel be!

105

TO PERENNA

When I thy parts run o'er, I can't espy
In any one, the least indecency;
But every line and limb diffused thence
A fair and unfamiliar excellence;
So that the more I look, the more I prove
There's still more cause why I the more should love.

106

TO OENONE.

What conscience, say, is it in thee,
When I a heart had one, [won]
To take away that heart from me,
And to retain thy own?

For shame or pity, now incline
To play a loving part;
Either to send me kindly thine,
Or give me back my heart.

Covet not both; but if thou dost

Resolve to part with neither;
Why! yet to shew that thou art just,
Take me and mine together.

107

TO ELECTRA

I dare not ask a kiss,
I dare not beg a smile;
Lest having that, or this,
I might grow proud the while.

No, no, the utmost share
Of my desire shall be,
Only to kiss that air
That lately kissed thee,

108

TO ANTHEA, WHO MAY COMMAND HIM ANY THING

Bid me to live, and I will live
Thy Protestant to be;
Or bid me love, and I will give
A loving heart to thee.

A heart as soft, a heart as kind,
A heart as sound and free
As in the whole world thou canst find,
That heart I'll give to thee.

Bid that heart stay, and it will stay
To honour thy decree;
Or bid it languish quite away,
And't shall do so for thee.

Bid me to weep, and I will weep,
While I have eyes to see;
And having none, yet I will keep
A heart to weep for thee.

Bid me despair, and I'll despair,
Under that cypress tree;
Or bid me die, and I will dare
E'en death, to die for thee.

--Thou art my life, my love, my heart,
The very eyes of me;
And hast command of every part,
To live and die for thee.

109

ANTHEA'S RETRACTATION

Anthea laugh'd, and, fearing lest excess
Might stretch the cords of civil comeliness
She with a dainty blush rebuked her face,
And call'd each line back to his rule and space.

110

LOVE LIGHTLY PLEASED

Let fair or foul my mistress be,
Or low, or tall, she pleaseth me;
Or let her walk, or stand, or sit,
The posture her's, I'm pleased with it;
Or let her tongue be still, or stir
Graceful is every thing from her;
Or let her grant, or else deny,
My love will fit each history.

111

TO DIANEME

Give me one kiss,
And no more:
If so be, this
Makes you poor
To enrich you,
I'll restore
For that one, two-
Thousand score.

112

UPON HER EYES

Clear are her eyes,
Like purest skies;

Discovering from thence
A baby there
That turns each sphere,
Like an Intelligence.

113

UPON HER FEET

Her pretty feet
Like snails did creep
A little out, and then,
As if they played at Bo-peep,
Did soon draw in again.

114

UPON A DELAYING LADY

Come, come away
Or let me go;
Must I here stay
Because you're slow,
And will continue so;
--Troth, lady, no.

I scorn to be
A slave to state;
And since I'm free,
I will not wait,
Henceforth at such a rate,

For needy fate.

If you desire
My spark should glow,
The peeping fire
You must blow;
Or I shall quickly grow
To frost, or snow.

115

THE CRUEL MAID

--AND, cruel maid, because I see
You scornful of my love, and me,
I'll trouble you no more, but go
My way, where you shall never know
What is become of me; there I
Will find me out a path to die,
Or learn some way how to forget
You and your name for ever;--yet
Ere I go hence, know this from me,
What will in time your fortune be;
This to your coyness I will tell;
And having spoke it once, Farewell.
--The lily will not long endure,
Nor the snow continue pure;
The rose, the violet, one day
See both these lady-flowers decay;
And you must fade as well as they.
And it may chance that love may turn,
And, like to mine, make your heart burn

And weep to see't; yet this thing do,
That my last vow commends to you;
When you shall see that I am dead,
For pity let a tear be shed;
And, with your mantle o'er me cast,
Give my cold lips a kiss at last;
If twice you kiss, you need not fear
That I shall stir or live more here.
Next hollow out a tomb to cover
Me, me, the most despised lover;
And write thereon, THIS, READER, KNOW;
LOVE KILL'D THIS MAN. No more, but so.

116

TO HIS MISTRESS, OBJECTING TO HIM NEITHER
TOYING OR TALKING

You say I love not, 'cause I do not play
Still with your curls, and kiss the time away.
You blame me, too, because I can't devise
Some sport, to please those babies in your eyes;
By Love's religion, I must here confess it,
The most I love, when I the least express it.
Shall griefs find tongues; full casks are ever found
To give, if any, yet but little sound.
Deep waters noiseless are; and this we know,
That chiding streams betray small depth below.
So when love speechless is, she doth express
A depth in love, and that depth bottomless.
Now, since my love is tongueless, know me such,
Who speak but little, 'cause I love so much.

117

IMPOSSIBILITIES: TO HIS FRIEND

My faithful friend, if you can see
The fruit to grow up, or the tree;
If you can see the colour come
Into the blushing pear or plum;
If you can see the water grow
To cakes of ice, or flakes of snow;
If you can see that drop of rain
Lost in the wild sea once again;
If you can see how dreams do creep
Into the brain by easy sleep:--
--Then there is hope that you may see
Her love me once, who now hates me.

118

THE BUBBLE: A SONG

To my revenge, and to her desperate fears,
Fly, thou made bubble of my sighs and tears!
In the wild air, when thou hast roll'd about,
And, like a blasting planet, found her out;
Stoop, mount, pass by to take her eye--then glare
Like to a dreadful comet in the air:
Next, when thou dost perceive her fixed sight
For thy revenge to be most opposite,
Then, like a globe, or ball of wild-fire, fly,

And break thyself in shivers on her eye!

119

DELIGHT IN DISORDER

A sweet disorder in the dress
Kindles in clothes a wantonness;
A lawn about the shoulders thrown
Into a fine distraction;
An erring lace, which here and there
Enthrals the crimson stomacher;
A cuff neglectful, and thereby
Ribbons to flow confusedly;
A winning wave, deserving note,
In the tempestuous petticoat;
A careless shoe-string, in whose tie
I see a wild civility;--
Do more bewitch me, than when art
Is too precise in every part.

120

TO SILVIA

Pardon my trespass, Silvia! I confess
My kiss out-went the bounds of shamefacedness:--
None is discreet at all times; no, not Jove
Himself, at one time, can be wise and love.

121

TO SILVIA TO WED

Let us, though late, at last, my Silvia, wed;
And loving lie in one devoted bed.
Thy watch may stand, my minutes fly post haste;
No sound calls back the year that once is past.
Then, sweetest Silvia, let's no longer stay;
True love, we know, precipitates delay.
Away with doubts, all scruples hence remove!
No man, at one time, can be wise, and love.

122

BARLEY-BREAK; OR, LAST IN HELL

We two are last in hell; what may we fear
To be tormented or kept pris'ners here I
Alas! if kissing be of plagues the worst,
We'll wish in hell we had been last and first.

123

ON A PERFUMED LADY

You say you're sweet: how should we know
Whether that you be sweet or no?
--From powders and perfumes keep free;
Then we shall smell how sweet you be!

124

THE PARCAE; OR, THREE DAINTY DESTINIES:
THE ARMILET

Three lovely sisters working were,
As they were closely set,
Of soft and dainty maiden-hair,
A curious Armilet.
I, smiling, ask'd them what they did,
Fair Destinies all three?
Who told me they had drawn a thread
Of life, and 'twas for me.
They shew'd me then how fine 'twas spun
And I replied thereto;
'I care not now how soon 'tis done,
Or cut, if cut by you.'

125

A CONJURATION: TO ELECTRA

By those soft tods of wool,
With which the air is full;
By all those tinctures there
That paint the hemisphere;
By dews and drizzling rain,
That swell the golden grain;
By all those sweets that be
I'th' flowery nunnery;
By silent nights, and the

Three forms of Hecate;
By all aspects that bless
The sober sorceress,
While juice she strains, and pith
To make her philtres with;
By Time, that hastens on
Things to perfection;
And by your self, the best
Conjurement of the rest;
--O, my Electra! be
In love with none but me.

126

TO SAPHO

Sapho, I will chuse to go
Where the northern winds do blow
Endless ice, and endless snow;
Rather than I once would see
But a winter's face in thee,--
To benumb my hopes and me.

127

OF LOVE: A SONNET

How Love came in, I do not know,
Whether by th'eye, or ear, or no;
Or whether with the soul it came,
At first, infused with the same;

Whether in part 'tis here or there,
Or, like the soul, whole every where.
This troubles me; but I as well
As any other, this can tell;
That when from hence she does depart,
The outlet then is from the heart.

128

TO DIANEME

Sweet, be not proud of those two eyes,
Which, star-like, sparkle in their skies;
Nor be you proud, that you can see
All hearts your captives, yours, yet free;
Be you not proud of that rich hair
Which wantons with the love-sick air;
Whenas that ruby which you wear,
Sunk from the tip of your soft ear,
Will last to be a precious stone,
When all your world of beauty's gone.

129

TO DIANEME

Dear, though to part it be a hell,
Yet, Dianeme, now farewell!
Thy frown last night did bid me go,
But whither, only grief does know.
I do beseech thee, ere we part,

(If merciful, as fair thou art;
Or else desir'st that maids should tell
Thy pity by Love's chronicle)
O, Dianeme, rather kill
Me, than to make me languish still!
'Tis cruelty in thee to th' height,
Thus, thus to wound, not kill outright;
Yet there's a way found, if thou please,
By sudden death, to give me ease;
And thus devised,--do thou but this,
--Bequeath to me one parting kiss!
So sup'rabundant joy shall be
The executioner of me.

130

KISSING USURY

Biancha, let
Me pay the debt
I owe thee for a kiss
Thou lend'st to me;
And I to thee
Will render ten for this.

If thou wilt say,
Ten will not pay
For that so rich a one;
I'll clear the sum,
If it will come
Unto a million.

He must of right,
To th' utmost mite,
Make payment for his pleasure,
(By this I guess)
Of happiness
Who has a little measure.

131

UPON THE LOSS OF HIS MISTRESSES

I have lost, and lately, these
Many dainty mistresses:--
Stately Julia, prime of all;
Sapho next, a principal:
Smooth Anthea, for a skin
White, and heaven-like crystalline:
Sweet Electra, and the choice
Myrha, for the lute and voice.
Next, Corinna, for her wit,
And the graceful use of it;
With Perilla:--All are gone;
Only Herrick's left alone,
For to number sorrow by
Their departures hence, and die.

132

THE WOUNDED HEART

Come, bring your sampler, and with art

Draw in't a wounded heart,
And dropping here and there;
Not that I think that any dart
Can make your's bleed a tear,
Or pierce it any where;
Yet do it to this end,--that I
May by
This secret see,
Though you can make
That heart to bleed, your's ne'er will ache
For me,

133

HIS MISTRESS TO HIM AT HIS FAREWELL

You may vow I'll not forget
To pay the debt
Which to thy memory stands as due
As faith can seal it you.
--Take then tribute of my tears;
So long as I have fears
To prompt me, I shall ever
Languish and look, but thy return see never.
Oh then to lessen my despair,
Print thy lips into the air,
So by this
Means, I may kiss thy kiss,
Whenas some kind
Wind
Shall hither waft it:--And, in lieu,
My lips shall send a thousand back to you.

134

CRUTCHES

Thou see'st me, Lucia, this year droop;
Three zodiacs fill'd more, I shall stoop;
Let crutches then provided be
To shore up my debility:
Then, while thou laugh'st, I'll sighing cry,
A ruin underpropt am I:
Don will I then my beadsman's gown;
And when so feeble I am grown
As my weak shoulders cannot bear
The burden of a grasshopper;
Yet with the bench of aged sires,
When I and they keep termly fires,
With my weak voice I'll sing, or say
Some odes I made of Lucia;--
Then will I heave my wither'd hand
To Jove the mighty, for to stand
Thy faithful friend, and to pour down
Upon thee many a benison.

135

TO ANTHEA

Anthea, I am going hence
With some small stock of innocence;
But yet those blessed gates I see

Withstanding entrance unto me;
To pray for me do thou begin;--
The porter then will let me in.

136

TO ANTHEA

Now is the time when all the lights wax dim;
And thou, Anthea, must withdraw from him
Who was thy servant: Dearest, bury me
Under that holy-oak, or gospel-tree;
Where, though thou see'st not, thou may'st think upon
Me, when thou yearly go'st procession;
Or, for mine honour, lay me in that tomb
In which thy sacred reliques shall have room;
For my embalming, Sweetest, there will be
No spices wanting, when I'm laid by thee.

137

TO HIS LOVELY MISTRESSES

One night i'th' year, my dearest Beauties, come,
And bring those dew-drink-offerings to my tomb;
When thence ye see my reverend ghost to rise,
And there to lick th' effused sacrifice,
Though paleness be the livery that I wear,
Look ye not wan or colourless for fear.
Trust me, I will not hurt ye, or once show
The least grim look, or cast a frown on you;

Nor shall the tapers, when I'm there, burn blue.
This I may do, perhaps, as I glide by,--
Cast on my girls a glance, and loving eye;
Or fold mine arms, and sigh, because I've lost
The world so soon, and in it, you the most:
--Than these, no fears more on your fancies fall,
Though then I smile, and speak no words at all.

138

TO PERILLA

Ah, my Perilla! dost thou grieve to see
Me, day by day, to steal away from thee?
Age calls me hence, and my gray hairs bid come,
And haste away to mine eternal home;
'Twill not be long, Perilla, after this,
That I must give thee the supremest kiss:--
Dead when I am, first cast in salt, and bring
Part of the cream from that religious spring,
With which, Perilla, wash my hands and feet;
That done, then wind me in that very sheet
Which wrapt thy smooth limbs, when thou didst implore
The Gods' protection, but the night before;
Follow me weeping to my turf, and there
Let fall a primrose, and with it a tear:
Then lastly, let some weekly strewings be
Devoted to the memory of me;
Then shall my ghost not walk about, but keep
Still in the cool and silent shades of sleep.

139

A MEDITATION FOR HIS MISTRESS

You are a Tulip seen to-day,
But, Dearest, of so short a stay,
That where you grew, scarce man can say.

You are a lovely July-flower;
Yet one rude wind, or ruffling shower,
Will force you hence, and in an hour.

You are a sparkling Rose i'th' bud,
Yet lost, ere that chaste flesh and blood
Can show where you or grew or stood.

You are a full-spread fair-set Vine,
And can with tendrils love entwine;
Yet dried, ere you distil your wine.

You are like Balm, enclosed well
In amber, or some crystal shell;
Yet lost ere you transfuse your smell.

You are a dainty Violet;
Yet wither'd, ere you can be set
Within the virgins coronet.

You are the Queen all flowers among;
But die you must, fair maid, ere long,
As he, the maker of this song.

140

TO THE VIRGINS, TO MAKE MUCH OF TIME

Gather ye rose-buds while ye may:
Old Time is still a-flying;
And this same flower that smiles to-day,
To-morrow will be dying.

The glorious lamp of heaven, the Sun,
The higher he's a-getting,
The sooner will his race be run,
And nearer he's to setting.

That age is best, which is the first,
When youth and blood are warmer;
But being spent, the worse, and worst
Times, still succeed the former.

--Then be not coy, but use your time,
And while ye may, go marry;
For having lost but once your prime,
You may for ever tarry.

** EPIGRAMS **

141

POSTING TO PRINTING

Let others to the printing-press run fast;

Since after death comes glory, I'll not haste.

142

HIS LOSS

All has been plunder'd from me but my wit:
Fortune herself can lay no claim to it.

143

THINGS MORTAL STILL MUTABLE

Things are uncertain; and the more we get,
The more on icy pavements we are set.

144

NO MAN WITHOUT MONEY

No man such rare parts hath, that he can swim,
If favour or occasion help not him.

145

THE PRESENT TIME BEST PLEASETH

Praise, they that will, times past: I joy to see
Myself now live; this age best pleaseth me!

146

WANT

Want is a softer wax, that takes thereon,
This, that, and every base impression,

147

SATISFACTION FOR SUFFERINGS

For all our works a recompence is sure;
'Tis sweet to think on what was hard t'endure.

148

WRITING

When words we want, Love teacheth to indite;
And what we blush to speak, she bids us write.

149

THE DEFINITION OF BEAUTY

Beauty no other thing is, than a beam
Flash'd out between the middle and extreme.

150

A MEAN IN OUR MEANS

Though frankincense the deities require,
We must not give all to the hallow'd fire.
Such be our gifts, and such be our expense,
As for ourselves to leave some frankincense.

151

MONEY MAKES THE MIRTH

When all birds else do of their music fail,
Money's the still-sweet-singing nightingale!

152

TEARS AND LAUGHTER

Knew'st thou one month would take thy life away,
Thou'dst weep; but laugh, should it not last a day.

153

UPON TEARS

Tears, though they're here below the sinner's brine,
Above, they are the Angels' spiced wine.

154

ON LOVE

Love's of itself too sweet; the best of all
Is, when love's honey has a dash of gall.

155

PEACE NOT PERMANENT

Great cities seldom rest; if there be none
T' invade from far, they'll find worse foes at home.

156

PARDONS

Those ends in war the best contentment bring,
Whose peace is made up with a pardoning.

157

TRUTH AND ERROR

Twixt truth and error, there's this difference known
Error is fruitful, truth is only one.

158

WIT PUNISHED PROSPERS MOST

Dread not the shackles; on with thine intent,
Good wits get more fame by their punishment.

159

BURIAL

Man may want land to live in; but for all
Nature finds out some place for burial.

160

NO PAINS, NO GAINS

If little labour, little are our gains;
Man's fortunes are according to his pains.

161

TO YOUTH

Drink wine, and live here blitheful while ye may;
The morrow's life too late is; Live to-day.

162

TO ENJOY THE TIME

While fates permit us, let's be merry;
Pass all we must the fatal ferry;
And this our life, too, whirls away,
With the rotation of the day.

163

FELICITY QUICK OF FLIGHT

Every time seems short to be
That's measured by felicity;
But one half-hour that's made up here
With grief, seems longer than a year.

164

MIRTH

True mirth resides not in the smiling skin;
The sweetest solace is to act no sin.

165

THE HEART

In prayer the lips ne'er act the winning part

Without the sweet concurrence of the heart.

166

LOVE, WHAT IT IS

Love is a circle, that doth restless move
In the same sweet eternity of Love.

167

DREAMS

Here we are all, by day; by night we're hurl'd
By dreams, each one into a several world.

168

AMBITION

In man, ambition is the common'st thing;
Each one by nature loves to be a king.

169

SAFETY ON THE SHORE

What though the sea be calm? Trust to the shore;
Ships have been drown'd, where late they danced before.

170

UPON A PAINTED GENTLEWOMAN

Men say you're fair; and fair ye are, 'tis true;
But, hark! we praise the painter now, not you.

171

UPON WRINKLES

Wrinkles no more are, or no less,
Than beauty turn'd to sourness.

172

CASUALTIES

Good things, that come of course, far less do please
Than those which come by sweet contingencies.

173

TO LIVE FREELY

Let's live in haste; use pleasures while we may;
Could life return, 'twould never lose a day.

174

NOTHING FREE-COST

Nothing comes free-cost here; Jove will not let
His gifts go from him, if not bought with sweat.

175

MAN'S DYING-PLACE UNCERTAIN

Man knows where first he ships himself; but he
Never can tell where shall his landing be.

176

LOSS FROM THE LEAST

Great men by small means oft are overthrown;
He's lord of thy life, who contemns his own.

177

POVERTY AND RICHES

Who with a little cannot be content,
Endures an everlasting punishment.

178

UPON MAN

Man is composed here of a twofold part;
The first of nature, and the next of art;
Art presupposes nature; nature, she
Prepares the way for man's docility.

179

PURPOSES

No wrath of men, or rage of seas,
Can shake a just man's purposes;
No threats of tyrants, or the grim
Visage of them can alter him;
But what he doth at first intend,
That he holds firmly to the end.

180

FOUR THINGS MAKE US HAPPY HERE

Health is the first good lent to men;
A gentle disposition then:
Next, to be rich by no by-ways;
Lastly, with friends t' enjoy our days.

181

THE WATCH

Man is a watch, wound up at first, but never
Wound up again; Once down, he's down for ever.
The watch once down, all motions then do cease;
The man's pulse stopt, all passions sleep in peace.

182

UPON THE DETRACTER

I ask'd thee oft what poets thou hast read,
And lik'st the best? Still thou repli'st, The dead.
--I shall, ere long, with green turfs cover'd be;
Then sure thou'lt like, or thou wilt envy, me.

183

ON HIMSELF

Live by thy Muse thou shalt, when others die,
Leaving no fame to long posterity;
When monarchies trans-shifted are, and gone,
Here shall endure thy vast dominion.

** NATURE AND LIFE **

184

I CALL AND I CALL

I call, I call: who do ye call?
The maids to catch this cowslip ball!
But since these cowslips fading be,
Troth, leave the flowers, and maids, take me!
Yet, if that neither you will do,
Speak but the word, and I'll take you,

185

THE SUCCESSION OF THE FOUR SWEET MONTHS

First, April, she with mellow showers
Opens the way for early flowers;
Then after her comes smiling May,
In a more rich and sweet array;
Next enters June, and brings us more
Gems than those two that went before;
Then, lastly, July comes, and she
More wealth brings in than all those three.

186

TO BLOSSOMS

Fair pledges of a fruitful tree,
Why do ye fall so fast?
Your date is not so past,
But you may stay yet here a-while,
To blush and gently smile;

And go at last.

What, were ye born to be
An hour or half's delight;
And so to bid good-night?
'Twas pity Nature brought ye forth,
Merely to show your worth,
And lose you quite.

But you are lovely leaves, where we
May read how soon things have
Their end, though ne'er so brave:
And after they have shown their pride,
Like you, a-while;--they glide
Into the grave.

187

THE SHOWER OF BLOSSOMS

Love in a shower of blossoms came
Down, and half drown'd me with the same;
The blooms that fell were white and red;
But with such sweets commingled,
As whether (this) I cannot tell,
My sight was pleased more, or my smell;
But true it was, as I roll'd there,
Without a thought of hurt or fear,
Love turn'd himself into a bee,
And with his javelin wounded me;---
From which mishap this use I make;
Where most sweets are, there lies a snake;

Kisses and favours are sweet things;
But those have thorns, and these have stings.

188

TO THE ROSE: SONG

Go, happy Rose, and interwove
With other flowers, bind my Love.
Tell her, too, she must not be
Longer flowing, longer free,
That so oft has fetter'd me.

Say, if she's fretful, I have bands
Of pearl and gold, to bind her hands;
Tell her, if she struggle still,
I have myrtle rods at will,
For to tame, though not to kill.

Take thou my blessing thus, and go
And tell her this,--but do not so!--
Lest a handsome anger fly
Like a lightning from her eye,
And burn thee up, as well as I!

189

THE FUNERAL RITES OF THE ROSE

The Rose was sick, and smiling died;
And, being to be sanctified,

About the bed, there sighing stood
The sweet and flowery sisterhood.
Some hung the head, while some did bring,
To wash her, water from the spring;
Some laid her forth, while others wept,
But all a solemn fast there kept.
The holy sisters some among,
The sacred dirge and trental sung;
But ah! what sweets smelt everywhere,
As heaven had spent all perfumes there!
At last, when prayers for the dead,
And rites, were all accomplished,
They, weeping, spread a lawny loom,
And closed her up as in a tomb.

190

THE BLEEDING HAND;
OR THE SPRIG OF EGLANTINE GIVEN TO A MAID

From this bleeding hand of mine,
Take this sprig of Eglantine:
Which, though sweet unto your smell,
Yet the fretful briar will tell,
He who plucks the sweets, shall prove
Many thorns to be in love.

191

TO CARNATIONS: A SONG

Stay while ye will, or go,
And leave no scent behind ye:
Yet trust me, I shall know
The place where I may find ye.

Within my Lucia's cheek,
(Whose livery ye wear)
Play ye at hide or seek,
I'm sure to find ye there.

192

TO PANSIES

Ah, Cruel Love! must I endure
Thy many scorns, and find no cure?
Say, are thy medicines made to be
Helps to all others but to me?
I'll leave thee, and to Pansies come:
Comforts you'll afford me some:
You can ease my heart, and do
What Love could ne'er be brought unto.

193

HOW PANSIES OR HEARTS-EASE CAME FIRST

Frolic virgins once these were,
Overloving, living here;
Being here their ends denied
Ran for sweet-hearts mad, and died.

Love, in pity of their tears,
And their loss in blooming years,
For their restless here-spent hours,
Gave them hearts-ease turn'd to flowers.

194

WHY FLOWERS CHANGE COLOUR

These fresh beauties, we can prove,
Once were virgins, sick of love,
Turn'd to flowers: still in some,
Colours go and colours come.

195

THE PRIMROSE

Ask me why I send you here
This sweet Infanta of the year?
Ask me why I send to you
This Primrose, thus bepearl'd with dew?
I will whisper to your ears,--
The sweets of love are mixt with tears.

Ask me why this flower does show
So yellow-green, and sickly too?
Ask me why the stalk is weak
And bending, yet it doth not break?
I will answer,--these discover
What fainting hopes are in a lover.

196

TO PRIMROSES FILLED WITH MORNING DEW

Why do ye weep, sweet babes? can tears
Speak grief in you,
Who were but born
just as the modest morn
Teem'd her refreshing dew?
Alas, you have not known that shower
That mars a flower,
Nor felt th' unkind
Breath of a blasting wind,
Nor are ye worn with years;
Or warp'd as we,
Who think it strange to see,
Such pretty flowers, like to orphans young,
To speak by tears, before ye have a tongue.

Speak, whimp'ring younglings, and make known
The reason why
Ye droop and weep;
Is it for want of sleep,
Or childish lullaby?
Or that ye have not seen as yet
The violet?
Or brought a kiss
From that Sweet-heart, to this?
--No, no, this sorrow shown
By your tears shed,
Would have this lecture read,

That things of greatest, so of meanest worth,
Conceived with grief are, and with tears brought forth.

197

TO DAISIES, NOT TO SHUT SO SOON

Shut not so soon; the dull-eyed night
Has not as yet begun
To make a seizure on the light,
Or to seal up the sun.

No marigolds yet closed are,
No shadows great appear;
Nor doth the early shepherds' star
Shine like a spangle here.

Stay but till my Julia close
Her life-begetting eye;
And let the whole world then dispose
Itself to live or die.

198

TO DAFFADILS

Fair Daffadils, we weep to see
You haste away so soon;
As yet the early-rising sun
Has not attain'd his noon.
Stay, stay,

Until the hasting day
Has run
But to the even-song;
And, having pray'd together, we
Will go with you along.

We have short time to stay, as you;
We have as short a spring;
As quick a growth to meet decay,
As you, or any thing.
We die
As your hours do, and dry
Away,
Like to the summer's rain;
Or as the pearls of morning's dew,
Ne'er to be found again.

199

TO VIOLETS

Welcome, maids of honour,
You do bring
In the Spring;
And wait upon her.

She has virgins many,
Fresh and fair;
Yet you are
More sweet than any.

You're the maiden posies;

And so graced,
To be placed
'Fore damask roses.

--Yet, though thus respected,
By and by
Ye do lie,
Poor girls, neglected.

200

THE APRON OF FLOWERS

To gather flowers, Sappha went,
And homeward she did bring
Within her lawny continent,
The treasure of the Spring.

She smiling blush'd, and blushing smiled,
And sweetly blushing thus,
She look'd as she'd been got with child
By young Favonius.

Her apron gave, as she did pass,
An odour more divine,
More pleasing too, than ever was
The lap of Proserpine.

201

THE LILY IN A CRYSTAL

You have beheld a smiling rose
When virgins' hands have drawn
O'er it a cobweb-lawn:
And here, you see, this lily shows,
Tomb'd in a crystal stone,
More fair in this transparent case
Than when it grew alone,
And had but single grace.

You see how cream but naked is,
Nor dances in the eye
Without a strawberry;
Or some fine tincture, like to this,
Which draws the sight thereto,
More by that wantoning with it,
Than when the paler hue
No mixture did admit.

You see how amber through the streams
More gently strokes the sight,
With some conceal'd delight,
Than when he darts his radiant beams
Into the boundless air;
Where either too much light his worth
Doth all at once impair,
Or set it little forth.

Put purple grapes or cherries in-
To glass, and they will send
More beauty to commend
Them, from that clean and subtle skin,
Than if they naked stood,

And had no other pride at all,
But their own flesh and blood,
And tinctures natural.

Thus lily, rose, grape, cherry, cream,
And strawberry do stir
More love, when they transfer
A weak, a soft, a broken beam;
Than if they should discover
At full their proper excellence,
Without some scene cast over,
To juggle with the sense.

Thus let this crystall'd lily be
A rule, how far to teach
Your nakedness must reach;
And that no further than we see
Those glaring colours laid
By art's wise hand, but to this end
They should obey a shade,
Lest they too far extend.

--So though you're white as swan or snow,
And have the power to move
A world of men to love;
Yet, when your lawns and silks shall flow,
And that white cloud divide
Into a doubtful twilight;--then,
Then will your hidden pride
Raise greater fires in men.

202

TO MEADOWS

Ye have been fresh and green,
Ye have been fill'd with flowers;
And ye the walks have been
Where maids have spent their hours.

You have beheld how they
With wicker arks did come,
To kiss and bear away
The richer cowslips home.

You've heard them sweetly sing,
And seen them in a round;
Each virgin, like a spring,
With honeysuckles crown'd.

But now, we see none here,
Whose silvery feet did tread
And with dishevell'd hair
Adorn'd this smoother mead.

Like unthrifts, having spent
Your stock, and needy grown
You're left here to lament
Your poor estates alone.

203

TO A GENTLEWOMAN, OBJECTING TO HIM HIS
GRAY HAIRS

Am I despised, because you say;
And I dare swear, that I am gray?
Know, Lady, you have but your day!
And time will come when you shall wear
Such frost and snow upon your hair;
And when, though long, it comes to pass,
You question with your looking-glass,
And in that sincere crystal seek
But find no rose-bud in your cheek,
Nor any bed to give the shew
Where such a rare carnation grew:-
Ah! then too late, close in your chamber keeping,
It will be told
That you are old,--
By those true tears you're weeping.

204

THE CHANGES: TO CORINNA

Be not proud, but now incline
Your soft ear to discipline;
You have changes in your life,
Sometimes peace, and sometimes strife;
You have ebbs of face and flows,
As your health or comes or goes;
You have hopes, and doubts, and fears,
Numberless as are your hairs;
You have pulses that do beat
High, and passions less of heat;
You are young, but must be old:--

And, to these, ye must be told,
Time, ere long, will come and plow
Loathed furrows in your brow:
And the dimness of your eye
Will no other thing imply,
But you must die
As well as I.

205

UPON MRS ELIZ. WHEELER, UNDER THE NAME OF AMARILLIS

Sweet Amarillis, by a spring's
Soft and soul-melting murmurings,
Slept; and thus sleeping, thither flew
A Robin-red-breast; who at view,
Not seeing her at all to stir,
Brought leaves and moss to cover her:
But while he, perking, there did pry
About the arch of either eye,
The lid began to let out day,--
At which poor Robin flew away;
And seeing her not dead, but all disleaved,
He chirpt for joy, to see himself deceived.

206

NO FAULT IN WOMEN

No fault in women, to refuse

The offer which they most would chuse.
--No fault: in women, to confess
How tedious they are in their dress;
--No fault in women, to lay on
The tincture of vermilion;
And there to give the cheek a dye
Of white, where Nature doth deny.
--No fault in women, to make show
Of largeness, when they're nothing so;
When, true it is, the outside swells
With inward buckram, little else.
--No fault in women, though they be
But seldom from suspicion free;
--No fault in womankind at all,
If they but slip, and never fall.

207

THE BAG OF THE BEE

About the sweet bag of a bee
Two Cupids fell at odds;
And whose the pretty prize should be
They vow'd to ask the Gods.

Which Venus hearing, thither came,
And for their boldness stript them;
And taking thence from each his flame,
With rods of myrtle whipt them.

Which done, to still their wanton cries,
When quiet grown she'd seen them,

She kiss'd and wiped their dove-like eyes,
And gave the bag between them.

208

THE PRESENT; OR, THE BAG OF THE BEE:

Fly to my mistress, pretty pilfering bee,
And say thou bring'st this honey-bag from me;
When on her lip thou hast thy sweet dew placed,
Mark if her tongue but slyly steal a taste;
If so, we live; if not, with mournful hum,
Toll forth my death; next, to my burial come.

209

TO THE WATER-NYMPHS DRINKING AT THE FOUNTAIN

Reach with your whiter hands to me
Some crystal of the spring;
And I about the cup shall see
Fresh lilies flourishing.

Or else, sweet nymphs, do you but this--
To th' glass your lips incline;
And I shall see by that one kiss
The water turn'd to wine.

210

HOW SPRINGS CAME FIRST

These springs were maidens once that loved,
But lost to that they most approved:
My story tells, by Love they were
Turn'd to these springs which we see here:
The pretty whimpering that they make,
When of the banks their leave they take,
Tells ye but this, they are the same,
In nothing changed but in their name.

211

TO THE HANDSOME MISTRESS GRACE POTTER

As is your name, so is your comely face
Touch'd every where with such diffused grace,
As that in all that admirable round,
There is not one least solecism found;
And as that part, so every portion else
Keeps line for line with beauty's parallels.

212

A HYMN TO THE GRACES

When I love, as some have told
Love I shall, when I am old,
O ye Graces! make me fit
For the welcoming of it!

Clean my rooms, as temples be,
To entertain that deity;
Give me words wherewith to woo,
Suppling and successful too;
Winning postures; and withal,
Manners each way musical;
Sweetness to allay my sour
And unsmooth behaviour:
For I know you have the skill
Vines to prune, though not to kill;
And of any wood ye see,
You can make a Mercury.

213

A HYMN TO LOVE

I will confess
With cheerfulness,
Love is a thing so likes me,
That, let her lay
On me all day,
I'll kiss the hand that strikes me.

I will not, I,
Now blubb'ring cry,
It, ah! too late repents me
That I did fall
To love at all--
Since love so much contents me.

No, no, I'll be

In fetters free;
While others they sit wringing
Their hands for pain,
I'll entertain
The wounds of love with singing.

With flowers and wine,
And cakes divine,
To strike me I will tempt thee;
Which done, no more
I'll come before
Thee and thine altars empty.

214

UPON LOVE:
BY WAY OF QUESTION AND ANSWER

I bring ye love. QUES. What will love do?
ANS. Like, and dislike ye.
I bring ye love. QUES. What will love do?
ANS. Stroke ye, to strike ye.
I bring ye love. QUES. What will love do?
ANS. Love will be-fool ye.
I bring ye love. QUES. What will love do?
ANS. Heat ye, to cool ye.
I bring ye love. QUES. What will love do?
ANS. Love, gifts will send ye.
I bring ye love. QUES. What will love do?
ANS. Stock ye, to spend ye.
I bring ye love. QUES. What will love do?
ANS. Love will fulfil ye.

I bring ye love. QUES. What will love do?
ANS. Kiss ye, to kill ye.

215

LOVERS HOW THEY COME AND PART

A Gyges ring they bear about them still,
To be, and not seen when and where they will;
They tread on clouds, and though they sometimes fall,
They fall like dew, and make no noise at all:
So silently they one to th' other come,
As colours steal into the pear or plum,
And air-like, leave no pression to be seen
Where'er they met, or parting place has been.

216

THE KISS: A DIALOGUE

1 Among thy fancies, tell me this,
What is the thing we call a kiss?
2 I shall resolve ye what it is:--

It is a creature born and bred
Between the lips, all cherry-red,
By love and warm desires fed,--
CHOR. And makes more soft the bridal bed.

2 It is an active flame, that flies
First to the babies of the eyes,

And charms them there with lullabies,--
CHOR. And stills the bride, too, when she cries.

2 Then to the chin, the cheek, the ear,
It frisks and flies, now here, now there:
'Tis now far off, and then 'tis near,--
CHOR. And here, and there, and every where.

1 Has it a speaking virtue? 2 Yes.
1 How speaks it, say? 2 Do you but this,--
Part your join'd lips, then speaks your kiss;
CHOR. And this Love's sweetest language is.

1 Has it a body? 2 Ay, and wings,
With thousand rare encolourings;
And as it flies, it gently sings--
CHOR. Love honey yields, but never stings.

217

COMFORT TO A YOUTH THAT HAD LOST HIS LOVE

What needs complaints,
When she a place
Has with the race
Of saints?
In endless mirth,
She thinks not on
What's said or done
In earth:
She sees no tears,
Or any tone

Of thy deep groan
She hears;
Nor does she mind,
Or think on't now,
That ever thou
Wast kind:--
But changed above,
She likes not there,
As she did here,
Thy love.
--Forbear, therefore,
And lull asleep
Thy woes, and weep
No more.

218

ORPHEUS

Orpheus he went, as poets tell,
To fetch Eurydice from hell;
And had her, but it was upon
This short, but strict condition;
Backward he should not look, while he
Led her through hell's obscurity.
But ah! it happen'd, as he made
His passage through that dreadful shade,
Revolve he did his loving eye,
For gentle fear or jealousy;
And looking back, that look did sever
Him and Eurydice for ever.

219

A REQUEST TO THE GRACES

Ponder my words, if so that any be
Known guilty here of incivility;
Let what is graceless, discomposed, and rude,
With sweetness, smoothness, softness be endued:
Teach it to blush, to curtsey, lisp, and show
Demure, but yet full of temptation, too.
Numbers ne'er tickle, or but lightly please,
Unless they have some wanton carriages:--
This if ye do, each piece will here be good
And graceful made by your neat sisterhood.

220

A HYMN TO VENUS AND CUPID

Sea-born goddess, let me be
By thy son thus graced, and thee,
That whene'er I woo, I find
Virgins coy, but not unkind.
Let me, when I kiss a maid,
Taste her lips, so overlaid
With love's sirop, that I may
In your temple, when I pray,
Kiss the altar, and confess
There's in love no bitterness.

221

TO BACCHUS: A CANTICLE

Whither dost thou hurry me,
Bacchus, being full of thee?
This way, that way, that way, this,--
Here and there a fresh Love is;
That doth like me, this doth please;
--Thus a thousand mistresses
I have now: yet I alone,
Having all, enjoy not one!

222

A HYMN TO BACCHUS

Bacchus, let me drink no more!
Wild are seas that want a shore!
When our drinking has no stint,
There is no one pleasure in't.
I have drank up for to please
Thee, that great cup, Hercules.
Urge no more; and there shall be
Daffadils giv'n up to thee.

223

A CANTICLE TO APOLLO

Play, Phoebus, on thy lute,

And we will sit all mute;
By listening to thy lyre,
That sets all ears on fire.

Hark, hark! the God does play!
And as he leads the way
Through heaven, the very spheres,
As men, turn all to ears!

224

TO MUSIC, TO BECALM A SWEET SICK YOUTH

Charms, that call down the moon from out her sphere,
On this sick youth work your enchantments here!
Bind up his senses with your numbers, so
As to entrance his pain, or cure his woe.
Fall gently, gently, and a-while him keep
Lost in the civil wilderness of sleep:
That done, then let him, dispossess'd of pain,
Like to a slumbering bride, awake again.

225

TO MUSIC: A SONG

Music, thou queen of heaven, care-charming spell,
That strik'st a stillness into hell;
Thou that tam'st tigers, and fierce storms, that rise,
With thy soul-melting lullabies;
Fall down, down, down, from those thy chiming spheres

To charm our souls, as thou enchant'st our ears.

226

SOFT MUSIC

The mellow touch of music most doth wound
The soul, when it doth rather sigh, than sound.

227

TO MUSIC

Begin to charm, and as thou strok'st mine ears
With thine enchantment, melt me into tears.
Then let thy active hand scud o'er thy lyre,
And make my spirits frantic with the fire;
That done, sink down into a silvery strain,
And make me smooth as balm and oil again.

228

THE VOICE AND VIOL

Rare is the voice itself: but when we sing
To th' lute or viol, then 'tis ravishing.

229

TO MUSIC, TO BECALM HIS FEVER

Charm me asleep, and melt me so
With thy delicious numbers;
That being ravish'd, hence I go
Away in easy slumbers.
Ease my sick head,
And make my bed,
Thou Power that canst sever
From me this ill;--
And quickly still,
Though thou not kill
My fever.

Thou sweetly canst convert the same
From a consuming fire,
Into a gentle-licking flame,
And make it thus expire.
Then make me weep
My pains asleep,
And give me such reposes,
That I, poor I,
May think, thereby,
I live and die
'Mongst roses.

Fall on me like a silent dew,
Or like those maiden showers,
Which, by the peep of day, do strew
A baptism o'er the flowers.
Melt, melt my pains
With thy soft strains;
That having ease me given,

With full delight,
I leave this light,
And take my flight
For Heaven.

** MUSAE GRAVIORES **

230

A THANKSGIVING TO GOD, FOR HIS HOUSE

Lord, thou hast given me a cell,
Wherein to dwell;
A little house, whose humble roof
Is weather proof;
Under the spars of which I lie
Both soft and dry;
Where thou, my chamber for to ward,
Hast set a guard
Of harmless thoughts, to watch and keep
Me, while I sleep.
Low is my porch, as is my fate;
Both void of state;
And yet the threshold of my door
Is worn by th' poor,
Who thither come, and freely get
Good words, or meat.
Like as my parlour, so my hall
And kitchen's small;
A little buttery, and therein
A little bin,

Which keeps my little loaf of bread
Unchipt, unflead;
Some brittle sticks of thorn or briar
Make me a fire,
Close by whose living coal I sit,
And glow like it.
Lord, I confess too, when I dine,
The pulse is thine,
And all those other bits that be
There placed by thee;
The worts, the purslain, and the mess
Of water-cress,
Which of thy kindness thou hast sent;
And my content
Makes those, and my beloved beet,
To be more sweet.
'Tis thou that crown'st my glittering hearth
With guiltless mirth,
And giv'st me wassail bowls to drink,
Spiced to the brink.
Lord, 'tis thy plenty-dropping hand
That soils my land,
And giv'st me, for my bushel sown,
Twice ten for one;
Thou mak'st my teeming hen to lay
Her egg each day;
Besides, my healthful ewes to bear
Me twins each year;
The while the conduits of my kine
Run cream, for wine:
All these, and better, thou dost send
Me, to this end,--
That I should render, for my part,

A thankful heart;
Which, fired with incense, I resign,
As wholly thine;
--But the acceptance, that must be,
My Christ, by Thee.

231

MATINS, OR MORNING PRAYER

When with the virgin morning thou dost rise,
Crossing thyself come thus to sacrifice;
First wash thy heart in innocence; then bring
Pure hands, pure habits, pure, pure every thing.
Next to the altar humbly kneel, and thence
Give up thy soul in clouds of frankincense.
Thy golden censers fill'd with odours sweet
Shall make thy actions with their ends to meet.

232

GOOD PRECEPTS, OR COUNSEL

In all thy need, be thou possest
Still with a well prepared breast;
Nor let the shackles make thee sad;
Thou canst but have what others had.
And this for comfort thou must know,
Times that are ill won't still be so:
Clouds will not ever pour down rain;
A sullen day will clear again.

First, peals of thunder we must hear;
When lutes and harps shall stroke the ear.

233

PRAY AND PROSPER

First offer incense; then, thy field and meads
Shall smile and smell the better by thy beads.
The spangling dew dredged o'er the grass shall be
Turn'd all to mell and manna there for thee.
Butter of amber, cream, and wine, and oil,
Shall run as rivers all throughout thy soil.
Would'st thou to sincere silver turn thy mould?
--Pray once, twice pray; and turn thy ground to gold.

234

THE BELL-MAN

Along the dark and silent night,
With my lantern and my light
And the tinkling of my bell,
Thus I walk, and this I tell:
--Death and dreadfulness call on
To the general session;
To whose dismal bar, we there
All accounts must come to clear:
Scores of sins we've made here many;
Wiped out few, God knows, if any.
Rise, ye debtors, then, and fall

To make payment, while I call:
Ponder this, when I am gone:
--By the clock 'tis almost One.

235

UPON TIME

Time was upon
The wing, to fly away;
And I call'd on
Him but awhile to stay;
But he'd be gone,
For aught that I could say.

He held out then
A writing, as he went,
And ask'd me, when
False man would be content
To pay again
What God and Nature lent.

An hour-glass,
In which were sands but few,
As he did pass,
He shew'd,--and told me too
Mine end near was;--
And so away he flew.

236

MEN MIND NO STATE IN SICKNESS

That flow of gallants which approach
To kiss thy hand from out the coach;
That fleet of lackeys which do run
Before thy swift postilion;
Those strong-hoof'd mules, which we behold
Rein'd in with purple, pearl, and gold,
And shed with silver, prove to be
The drawers of the axle-tree;
Thy wife, thy children, and the state
Of Persian looms and antique plate:
--All these, and more, shall then afford
No joy to thee, their sickly lord.

237

LIFE IS THE BODY'S LIGHT

Life is the body's light; which, once declining,
Those crimson clouds i' th' cheeks and lips leave shining:-
Those counter-changed tabbies in the air,
The sun once set, all of one colour are:
So, when death comes, fresh tinctures lose their place,
And dismal darkness then doth smutch the face.

238

TO THE LADY CREWE, UPON THE DEATH OF HER CHILD

Why, Madam, will ye longer weep,

Whenas your baby's lull'd asleep?
And, pretty child, feels now no more
Those pains it lately felt before.

All now is silent; groans are fled;
Your child lies still, yet is not dead,
But rather like a flower hid here,
To spring again another year.

239

UPON A CHILD THAT DIED

Here she lies, a pretty bud,
Lately made of flesh and blood;
Who as soon fell fast asleep,
As her little eyes did peep.
--Give her strewings, but not stir
The earth, that lightly covers her.

240

UPON A CHILD

Here a pretty baby lies
Sung asleep with lullabies;
Pray be silent, and not stir
Th' easy earth that covers her.

241

AN EPITAPH UPON A CHILD

Virgins promised when I died,
That they would each primrose-tide
Duly, morn and evening, come,
And with flowers dress my tomb.
--Having promised, pay your debts
Maids, and here strew violets.

242

AN EPITAPH UPON A VIRGIN

Here a solemn fast we keep,
While all beauty lies asleep;
Hush'd be all things, no noise here
But the toning of a tear;
Or a sigh of such as bring
Cowslips for her covering.

243

UPON A MAID

Here she lies, in bed of spice,
Fair as Eve in paradise;
For her beauty, it was such,
Poets could not praise too much.
Virgins come, and in a ring
Her supremest REQUIEM sing;

Then depart, but see ye tread
Lightly, lightly o'er the dead.

244

THE DIRGE OF JEPHTHAH'S DAUGHTER:
SUNG BY THE VIRGINS

O thou, the wonder of all days!
O paragon, and pearl of praise!
O Virgin-martyr, ever blest
Above the rest
Of all the maiden-train! We come,
And bring fresh strewings to thy tomb.

Thus, thus, and thus, we compass round
Thy harmless and unhaunted ground;
And as we sing thy dirge, we will
The daffadil,
And other flowers, lay upon
The altar of our love, thy stone.

Thou wonder of all maids, liest here,
Of daughters all, the dearest dear;
The eye of virgins; nay, the queen
Of this smooth green,
And all sweet meads, from whence we get
The primrose and the violet.

Too soon, too dear did Jephthah buy,
By thy sad loss, our liberty;
His was the bond and cov'nant, yet

Thou paid'st the debt;
Lamented Maid! he won the day:
But for the conquest thou didst pay.

Thy father brought with him along
The olive branch and victor's song;
He slew the Ammonites, we know,
But to thy woe;
And in the purchase of our peace,
The cure was worse than the disease.

For which obedient zeal of thine,
We offer here, before thy shrine,
Our sighs for storax, tears for wine;
And to make fine
And fresh thy hearse-cloth, we will here
Four times bestrew thee every year.

Receive, for this thy praise, our tears;
Receive this offering of our hairs;
Receive these crystal vials, fill'd
With tears, distill'd
From teeming eyes; to these we bring,
Each maid, her silver filleting,

To gild thy tomb; besides, these cauls,
These laces, ribbons, and these falls,
These veils, wherewith we use to hide
The bashful bride,
When we conduct her to her groom;
All, all we lay upon thy tomb.

No more, no more, since thou art dead,

Shall we e'er bring coy brides to bed;
No more, at yearly festivals,
We, cowslip balls,
Or chains of columbines shall make,
For this or that occasion's sake.

No, no; our maiden pleasures be
Wrapt in the winding-sheet with thee;
'Tis we are dead, though not i' th' grave;
Or if we have
One seed of life left, 'tis to keep
A Lent for thee, to fast and weep.

Sleep in thy peace, thy bed of spice,
And make this place all paradise;
May sweets grow here, and smoke from hence
Fat frankincense;
Let balm and cassia send their scent
From out thy maiden-monument.

May no wolf howl, or screech owl stir
A wing about thy sepulchre!
No boisterous winds or storms come hither,
To starve or wither
Thy soft sweet earth; but, like a spring,
Love keep it ever flourishing.

May all shy maids, at wonted hours,
Come forth to strew thy tomb with flowers;
May virgins, when they come to mourn,
Male-incense burn
Upon thine altar; then return,
And leave thee sleeping in thy urn.

245

THE WIDOWS' TEARS; OR, DIRGE OF DORCAS

Come pity us, all ye who see
Our harps hung on the willow-tree;
Come pity us, ye passers-by,
Who see or hear poor widows' cry;
Come pity us, and bring your ears
And eyes to pity widows' tears.
CHOR. And when you are come hither,
Then we will keep
A fast, and weep
Our eyes out all together,

For Tabitha; who dead lies here,
Clean wash'd, and laid out for the bier.
O modest matrons, weep and wail!
For now the corn and wine must fail;
The basket and the bin of bread,
Wherewith so many souls were fed,
CHOR. Stand empty here for ever;
And ah! the poor,
At thy worn door,
Shall be relieved never.

Woe worth the time, woe worth the day,
That reft us of thee, Tabitha!
For we have lost, with thee, the meal,
The bits, the morsels, and the deal
Of gentle paste and yielding dough,

That thou on widows did bestow.
CHOR. All's gone, and death hath taken
Away from us
Our maundy; thus
Thy widows stand forsaken.

Ah, Dorcas, Dorcas! now adieu
We bid the cruise and pannier too;
Ay, and the flesh, for and the fish,
Doled to us in that lordly dish.
We take our leaves now of the loom
From whence the housewives' cloth did come;
CHOR. The web affords now nothing;
Thou being dead,
The worsted thread
Is cut, that made us clothing.

Farewell the flax and reaming wool,
With which thy house was plentiful;
Farewell the coats, the garments, and
The sheets, the rugs, made by thy hand;
Farewell thy fire and thy light,
That ne'er went out by day or night:--
CHOR. No, or thy zeal so speedy,
That found a way,
By peep of day,
To feed and clothe the needy.

But ah, alas! the almond-bough
And olive-branch is wither'd now;
The wine-press now is ta'en from us,
The saffron and the calamus;
The spice and spikenard hence is gone,

The storax and the cinnamon;
CHOR. The carol of our gladness
Has taken wing;
And our late spring
Of mirth is turn'd to sadness.

How wise wast thou in all thy ways!
How worthy of respect and praise!
How matron-like didst thou go drest!
How soberly above the rest
Of those that prank it with their plumes,
And jet it with their choice perfumes!
CHOR. Thy vestures were not flowing;
Nor did the street
Accuse thy feet
Of mincing in their going.

And though thou here liest dead, we see
A deal of beauty yet in thee.
How sweetly shews thy smiling face,
Thy lips with all diffused grace!
Thy hands, though cold, yet spotless, white,
And comely as the chrysolite.
CHOR. Thy belly like a hill is,
Or as a neat
Clean heap of wheat,
All set about with lilies.

Sleep with thy beauties here, while we
Will shew these garments made by thee;
These were the coats; in these are read
The monuments of Dorcas dead:
These were thy acts, and thou shalt have

These hung as honours o'er thy grave:--
CHOR. And after us, distressed,
Should fame be dumb,
Thy very tomb
Would cry out, Thou art blessed.

246

UPON HIS SISTER-IN-LAW, MISTRESS ELIZABETH HERRICK

First, for effusions due unto the dead,
My solemn vows have here accomplished;
Next, how I love thee, that my grief must tell,
Wherein thou liv'st for ever.--Dear, farewell!

247

TO HIS KINSWOMAN, MISTRESS SUSANNA HERRICK

When I consider, dearest, thou dost stay
But here awhile, to languish and decay;
Like to these garden glories, which here be
The flowery-sweet resemblances of thee:
With grief of heart, methinks, I thus do cry,
Would thou hadst ne'er been born, or might'st not die!

248

ON HIMSELF

I'll write no more of love, but now repent
Of all those times that I in it have spent.
I'll write no more of life, but wish 'twas ended,
And that my dust was to the earth commended.

249

HIS WISH TO PRIVACY

Give me a cell
To dwell,
Where no foot hath
A path;
There will I spend,
And end,
My wearied years
In tears.

250

TO HIS PATERNAL COUNTRY

O earth! earth! earth! hear thou my voice, and be
Loving and gentle for to cover me!
Banish'd from thee I live;--ne'er to return,
Unless thou giv'st my small remains an urn.

251

COCK-CROW

Bell-man of night, if I about shall go
For to deny my Master, do thou crow!
Thou stop'st Saint Peter in the midst of sin;
Stay me, by crowing, ere I do begin;
Better it is, premonish'd, for to shun
A sin, than fall to weeping when 'tis done.

252

TO HIS CONSCIENCE

Can I not sin, but thou wilt be
My private protonotary?
Can I not woo thee, to pass by
A short and sweet iniquity?
I'll cast a mist and cloud upon
My delicate transgression,
So utter dark, as that no eye
Shall see the hugg'd impiety.
Gifts blind the wise, and bribes do please
And wind all other witnesses;
And wilt not thou with gold be tied,
To lay thy pen and ink aside,
That in the mirk and tongueless night,
Wanton I may, and thou not write?
--It will not be: And therefore, now,
For times to come, I'll make this vow;
From aberrations to live free:
So I'll not fear the judge, or thee.

253

TO HEAVEN

Open thy gates
To him who weeping waits,
And might come in,
But that held back by sin.
Let mercy be
So kind, to set me free,
And I will straight
Come in, or force the gate.

254

AN ODE OF THE BIRTH OF OUR SAVIOUR

In numbers, and but these few,
I sing thy birth, oh JESU!
Thou pretty Baby, born here,
With sup'rabundant scorn here;
Who for thy princely port here,
Hadst for thy place
Of birth, a base
Out-stable for thy court here.

Instead of neat enclosures
Of interwoven osiers;
Instead of fragrant posies
Of daffadils and roses,
Thy cradle, kingly stranger,

As gospel tells,
Was nothing else,
But, here, a homely manger.

But we with silks, not cruels,
With sundry precious jewels,
And lily-work will dress thee;
And as we dispossess thee
Of clouts, we'll make a chamber,
Sweet babe, for thee,
Of ivory,
And plaster'd round with amber.

The Jews, they did disdain thee;
But we will entertain thee
With glories to await here,
Upon thy princely state here,
And more for love than pity:
From year to year
We'll make thee, here,
A free-born of our city.

255

TO HIS SAVIOUR, A CHILD;
A PRESENT, BY A CHILD

Go, pretty child, and bear this flower
Unto thy little Saviour;
And tell him, by that bud now blown,
He is the Rose of Sharon known.
When thou hast said so, stick it there

Upon his bib or stomacher;
And tell him, for good handsel too,
That thou hast brought a whistle new,
Made of a clean straight oaten reed,
To charm his cries at time of need;
Tell him, for coral, thou hast none,
But if thou hadst, he should have one;
But poor thou art, and known to be
Even as moneyless as he.
Lastly, if thou canst win a kiss
From those melifluous lips of his;--
Then never take a second on,
To spoil the first impression.

256

GRACE FOR A CHILD

Here, a little child, I stand,
Heaving up my either hand:
Cold as paddocks though they be,
Here I lift them up to thee,
For a benison to fall
On our meat, and on us all.
Amen.

257

HIS LITANY, TO THE HOLY SPIRIT

In the hour of my distress,

When temptations me oppress,
And when I my sins confess,
Sweet Spirit, comfort me!

When I lie within my bed,
Sick in heart, and sick in head,
And with doubts discomforted,
Sweet Spirit, comfort me!

When the house doth sigh and weep,
And the world is drown'd in sleep,
Yet mine eyes the watch do keep,
Sweet Spirit, comfort me!

When the artless doctor sees
No one hope, but of his fees,
And his skill runs on the lees,
Sweet Spirit, comfort me!

When his potion and his pill,
Has, or none, or little skill,
Meet for nothing but to kill,
Sweet Spirit, comfort me!

When the passing-bell doth toll,
And the furies in a shoal
Come to fright a parting soul,
Sweet Spirit, comfort me!

When the tapers now burn blue,
And the comforters are few,
And that number more than true,
Sweet Spirit, comfort me!

When the priest his last hath pray'd,
And I nod to what is said,
'Cause my speech is now decay'd,
Sweet Spirit, comfort me!

When, God knows, I'm tost about
Either with despair, or doubt;
Yet, before the glass be out,
Sweet Spirit, comfort me!

When the tempter me pursu'th
With the sins of all my youth,
And half damns me with untruth,
Sweet Spirit, comfort me!

When the flames and hellish cries
Fright mine ears, and fright mine eyes,
And all terrors me surprise,
Sweet Spirit, comfort me!

When the Judgment is reveal'd,
And that open'd which was seal'd;
When to Thee I have appeal'd,
Sweet Spirit, comfort me!

258

TO DEATH

Thou bidst me come away,
And I'll no longer stay,

Than for to shed some tears
For faults of former years;
And to repent some crimes
Done in the present times;
And next, to take a bit
Of bread, and wine with it;
To don my robes of love,
Fit for the place above;
To gird my loins about
With charity throughout;
And so to travel hence
With feet of innocence;
These done, I'll only cry,
'God, mercy!' and so die.

259

TO HIS SWEET SAVIOUR

Night hath no wings to him that cannot sleep;
And Time seems then not for to fly, but creep;
Slowly her chariot drives, as if that she
Had broke her wheel, or crack'd her axletree.
Just so it is with me, who list'ning, pray
The winds to blow the tedious night away,
That I might see the cheerful peeping day.
Sick is my heart; O Saviour! do Thou please
To make my bed soft in my sicknesses;
Lighten my candle, so that I beneath
Sleep not for ever in the vaults of death;
Let me thy voice betimes i' th' morning hear;
Call, and I'll come; say Thou the when and where:

Draw me but first, and after Thee I'll run,
And make no one stop till my race be done.

260

ETERNITY

O years! and age! farewell:
Behold I go,
Where I do know
Infinity to dwell.

And these mine eyes shall see
All times, how they
Are lost i' th' sea
Of vast eternity:--

Where never moon shall sway
The stars; but she,
And night, shall be
Drown'd in one endless day.

261

THE WHITE ISLAND:
OR PLACE OF THE BLEST

In this world, the Isle of Dreams,
While we sit by sorrow's streams,
Tears and terrors are our themes,
Reciting:

But when once from hence we fly,
More and more approaching nigh
Unto young eternity,
Uniting

In that whiter Island, where
Things are evermore sincere:
Candour here, and lustre there,
Delighting:--

There no monstrous fancies shall
Out of hell an horror call,
To create, or cause at all
Affrighting.

There, in calm and cooling sleep,
We our eyes shall never steep,
But eternal watch shall keep,
Attending

Pleasures such as shall pursue
Me immortalized, and you;
And fresh joys, as never too
Have ending.

www.bookjungle.com email: sales@bookjungle.com fax: 630-214-0564 mail: Book Jungle PO Box 2226 Champaign, IL 61825

The Codes Of Hammurabi And Moses
W. W. Davies

QTY

The discovery of the Hammurabi Code is one of the greatest achievements of archaeology, and is of paramount interest, not only to the student of the Bible, but also to all those interested in ancient history...

Religion ISBN: *1-59462-338-4* Pages:132 MSRP *$12.95*

The Theory of Moral Sentiments
Adam Smith

QTY

This work from 1749. contains original theories of conscience amd moral judgment and it is the foundation for systemof morals.

Philosophy ISBN: *1-59462-777-0* Pages:536 MSRP *$19.95*

Jessica's First Prayer
Hesba Stretton

QTY

In a screened and secluded corner of one of the many railway-bridges which span the streets of London there could be seen a few years ago, from five o'clock every morning until half past eight, a tidily set-out coffee-stall, consisting of a trestle and board, upon which stood two large tin cans, with a small fire of charcoal burning under each so as to keep the coffee boiling during the early hours of the morning when the work-people were thronging into the city on their way to their daily toil...

Childrens ISBN: *1-59462-373-2* Pages:84 MSRP *$9.95*

My Life and Work
Henry Ford

QTY

Henry Ford revolutionized the world with his implementation of mass production for the Model T automobile. Gain valuable business insight into his life and work with his own auto-biography... "We have only started on our development of our country we have not as yet, with all our talk of wonderful progress, done more than scratch the surface. The progress has been wonderful enough but..."

Biographies/ ISBN: *1-59462-198-5* Pages:300 MSRP *$21.95*

www.bookjungle.com *email: sales@bookjungle.com fax: 630-214-0564 mail: Book Jungle PO Box 2226 Champaign, IL 61825*

The Art of Cross-Examination
Francis Wellman

QTY

I presume it is the experience of every author, after his first book is published upon an important subject, to be almost overwhelmed with a wealth of ideas and illustrations which could readily have been included in his book, and which to his own mind, at least, seem to make a second edition inevitable. Such certainly was the case with me; and when the first edition had reached its sixth impression in five months, I rejoiced to learn that it seemed to my publishers that the book had met with a sufficiently favorable reception to justify a second and considerably enlarged edition. ...

Reference   ISBN: *1-59462-647-2*   Pages:412   MSRP *$19.95*

On the Duty of Civil Disobedience
Henry David Thoreau

QTY

Thoreau wrote his famous essay, On the Duty of Civil Disobedience, as a protest against an unjust but popular war and the immoral but popular institution of slave-owning. He did more than write—he declined to pay his taxes, and was hauled off to gaol in consequence. Who can say how much this refusal of his hastened the end of the war and of slavery ?

Law   ISBN: *1-59462-747-9*   Pages:48   MSRP *$7.45*

Dream Psychology Psychoanalysis for Beginners
Sigmund Freud

QTY

Sigmund Freud, born Sigismund Schlomo Freud (May 6, 1856 - September 23, 1939), was a Jewish-Austrian neurologist and psychiatrist who co-founded the psychoanalytic school of psychology. Freud is best known for his theories of the unconscious mind, especially involving the mechanism of repression; his redefinition of sexual desire as mobile and directed towards a wide variety of objects; and his therapeutic techniques, especially his understanding of transference in the therapeutic relationship and the presumed value of dreams as sources of insight into unconscious desires.

Psychology   ISBN: *1-59462-905-6*   Pages:196   MSRP *$15.45*

The Miracle of Right Thought
Orison Swett Marden

QTY

Believe with all of your heart that you will do what you were made to do. When the mind has once formed the habit of holding cheerful, happy, prosperous pictures, it will not be easy to form the opposite habit. It does not matter how improbable or how far away this realization may see, or how dark the prospects may be, if we visualize them as best we can, as vividly as possible, hold tenaciously to them and vigorously struggle to attain them, they will gradually become actualized, realized in the life. But a desire, a longing without endeavor, a yearning abandoned or held indifferently will vanish without realization.

Self Help   ISBN: *1-59462-644-8*   Pages:360   MSRP *$25.45*

www.bookjungle.com email: sales@bookjungle.com fax: 630-214-0564 mail: Book Jungle PO Box 2226 Champaign, IL 61825

QTY

	Title	ISBN	Price
☐	**The Rosicrucian Cosmo-Conception Mystic Christianity** by *Max Heindel*	ISBN: 1-59462-188-8	$38.95
	The Rosicrucian Cosmo-conception is not dogmatic, neither does it appeal to any other authority than the reason of the student. It is: not controversial, but is: sent forth in the, hope that it may help to clear...	New Age/Religion Pages 646	
☐	**Abandonment To Divine Providence** by *Jean-Pierre de Caussade*	ISBN: 1-59462-228-0	$25.95
	"The Rev. Jean Pierre de Caussade was one of the most remarkable spiritual writers of the Society of Jesus in France in the 18th Century. His death took place at Toulouse in 1751. His works have gone through many editions and have been republished..."	Inspirational/Religion Pages 400	
☐	**Mental Chemistry** by *Charles Haanel*	ISBN: 1-59462-192-6	$23.95
	Mental Chemistry allows the change of material conditions by combining and appropriately utilizing the power of the mind. Much like applied chemistry creates something new and unique out of careful combinations of chemicals the mastery of mental chemistry...	New Age Pages 354	
☐	**The Letters of Robert Browning and Elizabeth Barret Barrett 1845-1846 vol II** by *Robert Browning* and *Elizabeth Barrett*	ISBN: 1-59462-193-4	$35.95
		Biographies Pages 596	
☐	**Gleanings In Genesis (volume I)** by *Arthur W. Pink*	ISBN: 1-59462-130-6	$27.45
	Appropriately has Genesis been termed "the seed plot of the Bible" for in it we have, in germ form, almost all of the great doctrines which are afterwards fully developed in the books of Scripture which follow...	Religion/Inspirational Pages 420	
☐	**The Master Key** by *L. W. de Laurence*	ISBN: 1-59462-001-6	$30.95
	In no branch of human knowledge has there been a more lively increase of the spirit of research during the past few years than in the study of Psychology. Concentration and Mental Discipline. The requests for authentic lessons in Thought Control, Mental Discipline and...	New Age/Business Pages 422	
☐	**The Lesser Key Of Solomon Goetia** by *L. W. de Laurence*	ISBN: 1-59462-092-X	$9.95
	This translation of the first book of the "Lemegton" which is now for the first time made accessible to students of Talismanic Magic was done, after careful collation and edition, from numerous Ancient Manuscripts in Hebrew, Latin, and French...	New Age/Occult Pages 92	
☐	**Rubaiyat Of Omar Khayyam** by *Edward Fitzgerald*	ISBN: 1-59462-332-5	$13.95
	Edward Fitzgerald, whom the world has already learned, in spite of his own efforts to remain within the shadow of anonymity, to look upon as one of the rarest poets of the century, was born at Bredfield, in Suffolk, on the 31st of March, 1809. He was the third son of John Purcell...	Music Pages 172	
☐	**Ancient Law** by *Henry Maine*	ISBN: 1-59462-128-4	$29.95
	The chief object of the following pages is to indicate some of the earliest ideas of mankind, as they are reflected in Ancient Law, and to point out the relation of those ideas to modern thought.	Religiom/History Pages 452	
☐	**Far-Away Stories** by *William J. Locke*	ISBN: 1-59462-129-2	$19.45
	"Good wine needs no bush, but a collection of mixed vintages does. And this book is just such a collection. Some of the stories I do not want to remain buried for ever in the museum files of dead magazine-numbers an author's not unpardonable vanity..."	Fiction Pages 272	
☐	**Life of David Crockett** by *David Crockett*	ISBN: 1-59462-250-7	$27.45
	"Colonel David Crockett was one of the most remarkable men of the times in which he lived. Born in humble life, but gifted with a strong will, an indomitable courage, and unremitting perseverance...	Biographies/New Age Pages 424	
☐	**Lip-Reading** by *Edward Nitchie*	ISBN: 1-59462-206-X	$25.95
	Edward B. Nitchie, founder of the New York School for the Hard of Hearing, now the Nitchie School of Lip-Reading, Inc, wrote "LIP-READING Principles and Practice". The development and perfecting of this meritorious work on lip-reading was an undertaking...	How-to Pages 400	
☐	**A Handbook of Suggestive Therapeutics, Applied Hypnotism, Psychic Science** by *Henry Munro*	ISBN: 1-59462-214-0	$24.95
		Health/New Age/Health/Self-help Pages 376	
☐	**A Doll's House: and Two Other Plays** by *Henrik Ibsen*	ISBN: 1-59462-112-8	$19.95
	Henrik Ibsen created this classic when in revolutionary 1848 Rome. Introducing some striking concepts in playwriting for the realist genre, this play has been studied the world over.	Fiction/Classics/Plays 308	
☐	**The Light of Asia** by *sir Edwin Arnold*	ISBN: 1-59462-204-3	$13.95
	In this poetic masterpiece, Edwin Arnold describes the life and teachings of Buddha. The man who was to become known as Buddha to the world was born as Prince Gautama of India but he rejected the worldly riches and abandoned the reigns of power when...	Religion/History/Biographies Pages 170	
☐	**The Complete Works of Guy de Maupassant** by *Guy de Maupassant*	ISBN: 1-59462-157-8	$16.95
	"For days and days, nights and nights, I had dreamed of that first kiss which was to consecrate our engagement, and I knew not on what spot I should put my lips..."	Fiction/Classics Pages 240	
☐	**The Art of Cross-Examination** by *Francis L. Wellman*	ISBN: 1-59462-309-0	$26.95
	Written by a renowned trial lawyer, Wellman imparts his experience and uses case studies to explain how to use psychology to extract desired information through questioning.	How-to/Science/Reference Pages 408	
☐	**Answered or Unanswered?** by *Louisa Vaughan*	ISBN: 1-59462-248-5	$10.95
	Miracles of Faith in China	Religion Pages 112	
☐	**The Edinburgh Lectures on Mental Science (1909)** by *Thomas*	ISBN: 1-59462-008-3	$11.95
	This book contains the substance of a course of lectures recently given by the writer in the Queen Street Hall, Edinburgh. Its purpose is to indicate the Natural Principles governing the relation between Mental Action and Material Conditions...	New Age/Psychology Pages 148	
☐	**Ayesha** by *H. Rider Haggard*	ISBN: 1-59462-301-5	$24.95
	Verily and indeed it is the unexpected that happens! Probably if there was one person upon the earth from whom the Editor of this, and of a certain previous history, did not expect to hear again...	Classics Pages 380	
☐	**Ayala's Angel** by *Anthony Trollope*	ISBN: 1-59462-352-X	$29.95
	The two girls were both pretty, but Lucy who was twenty-one who supposed to be simple and comparatively unattractive, whereas Ayala was credited, as her Bombwhat romantic name might show, with poetic charm and a taste for romance. Ayala when her father died was nineteen...	Fiction Pages 484	
☐	**The American Commonwealth** by *James Bryce*	ISBN: 1-59462-286-8	$34.45
	An interpretation of American democratic political theory. It examines political mechanics and society from the perspective of Scotsman James Bryce	Politics Pages 572	
☐	**Stories of the Pilgrims** by *Margaret P. Pumphrey*	ISBN: 1-59462-116-0	$17.95
	This book explores pilgrims religious oppression in England as well as their escape to Holland and eventual crossing to America on the Mayflower, and their early days in New England...	History Pages 268	

www.bookjungle.com email: sales@bookjungle.com fax: 630-214-0564 mail: Book Jungle PO Box 2226 Champaign, IL 61825

Title	ISBN	Price	QTY
The Fasting Cure by *Sinclair Upton*	1-59462-222-1	$13.95	
In the Cosmopolitan Magazine for May, 1910, and in the Contemporary Review (London) for April, 1910, I published an article dealing with my experiences in fasting. I have written a great many magazine articles, but never one which attracted so much attention... *New Age/Self Help/Health Pages 164*			
Hebrew Astrology by *Sepharial*	1-59462-308-2	$13.45	
In these days of advanced thinking it is a matter of common observation that we have left many of the old landmarks behind and that we are now pressing forward to greater heights and to a wider horizon than that which represented the mind-content of our progenitors... *Astrology Pages 144*			
Thought Vibration or The Law of Attraction in the Thought World by *William Walker Atkinson*	1-59462-127-6	$12.95	
Psychology/Religion Pages 144			
Optimism by *Helen Keller*	1-59462-108-X	$15.95	
Helen Keller was blind, deaf, and mute since 19 months old, yet famously learned how to overcome these handicaps, communicate with the world, and spread her lectures promoting optimism. An inspiring read for everyone... *Biographies/Inspirational Pages 84*			
Sara Crewe by *Frances Burnett*	1-59462-360-0	$9.45	
In the first place, Miss Minchin lived in London. Her home was a large, dull, tall one, in a large, dull square, where all the houses were alike, and all the sparrows were alike, and where all the door-knockers made the same heavy sound... *Childrens/Classic Pages 88*			
The Autobiography of Benjamin Franklin by *Benjamin Franklin*	1-59462-135-7	$24.95	
The Autobiography of Benjamin Franklin has probably been more extensively read than any other American historical work, and no other book of its kind has had such ups and downs of fortune. Franklin lived for many years in England, where he was agent... *Biographies/History Pages 332*			

Name	
Email	
Telephone	
Address	
City, State ZIP	

☐ Credit Card   ☐ Check / Money Order

Credit Card Number	
Expiration Date	
Signature	

Please Mail to: Book Jungle
                    PO Box 2226
                    Champaign, IL 61825
or Fax to: 630-214-0564

ORDERING INFORMATION

web: *www.bookjungle.com*
email: *sales@bookjungle.com*
fax: *630-214-0564*
mail: *Book Jungle PO Box 2226 Champaign, IL 61825*
or PayPal *to sales@bookjungle.com*

Please contact us for bulk discounts

DIRECT-ORDER TERMS

20% Discount if You Order Two or More Books
Free Domestic Shipping!
Accepted: Master Card, Visa, Discover, American Express

www.ingramcontent.com/pod-product-compliance
Lightning Source LLC
Chambersburg PA
CBHW080449170426
43196CB00016B/2732